Misguided By Mormonism

*Conversations with Former
Mormon Bishop Lee
and Kathy Baker
Discussing the Differences
Between Mormonism and
Biblical Christianity*

Christina R. Darlington
Director of Witnesses for Jesus, Inc.

MISGUIDED BY MORMONISM

ISBN: 1719114501
ISBN-13: 978-1719114509

DEDICATION

This book is dedicated to the Mormons and Christians we are helping through our website, video and radio ministry. Our hope is that this book will be a valuable resource for Bible-believing Christians to clarify the differences between Mormonism and Bible-based Christianity with their LDS friends and neighbors. We trust this book will serve as an additional support resource for anyone seeking spiritual recovery from the deception of Mormonism.

TABLE OF CONTENTS

INTRODUCTION

Since 1997, I, Christy Darlington, have directed the non-profit ministry, Witnesses for Jesus, which is dedicated to sharing the good news of the gospel of Jesus Christ with people lost in the deception of the Mormon and Jehovah's Witness faiths.

In 2011, former Mormon Bishop Lee Baker and his wife Kathy joined our ministry team as unpaid volunteers, living off of retirement, in order to help Mormons (also called, "Latter-day Saints" or "LDS") leave the counterfeit beliefs of Mormonism for a true faith in Jesus Christ as He is defined in the Bible. After helping thousands of people see the truth of Mormonism through their radio programs, Lee and Kathy Baker and I worked together to compile this book containing the text of our two-minute programs called, "Misguided by Mormonism," along with supporting documentation.

Realizing that people who leave Mormonism struggle with questions on what to believe, where to go, and who to trust, our goal in creating these radio programs and book is to contrast the history and beliefs of Mormonism with God's Word, the Bible, so that anyone reading this book will be able to leave Mormonism without losing their faith in Jesus Christ. Lee Baker writes,

"Kathy and I have been separated from the

1

Mormon Church for several years now. The depth and breadth of our understanding of the true message of the Bible and the true mission of Jesus Christ has brought us a lasting freedom and peace, never before experienced, even as an Active Bishop of the Mormon Church. We successfully have left our faith in Mormonism without losing our faith in Jesus Christ. This new and very personal relationship with Jesus Christ awaits you, if and when you move on the inspiration of the Holy Spirit of God to guide you as you search for the Truth."

Throughout this book, we reference Mormon beliefs that are not Christian. Mormons are often offended when their beliefs are called "non-Christian" because they hold to similar moral values and beliefs about Jesus Christ. But what determines whether a church is truly Christian is whether its beliefs agree with the fundamental teachings of Christianity (as discussed in the historic Christian creeds), and whether their beliefs are supported by the teachings of the Bible. So any unique belief that has no support from the historic Christian creeds and is not biblical (that is, it is not found in the teachings of the Bible or is contradicted by the Bible), should be rejected by all Bible-believing Christians as a non-Christian belief. As we will discuss in this book, Mormonism denies many of the foundational teachings of Christianity and cannot be called "Christian."

On November 20, 2013, the Mormon Church published an essay on lds.org entitled, "**Are Mormons Christian?**." They state,

> "In recent decades, however, **some have claimed that The Church of Jesus Christ of Latter-day Saints is not a Christian church**. The most oft-used reasons are the following:
>
> 1. **Latter-day Saints do not accept the creeds,** confessions, and formulations of post–New Testament Christianity.
>
> 2. **The Church of Jesus Christ of Latter-day Saints does not descend through the historical line of traditional Christianity**. That is, Latter-day Saints are not Roman Catholic, Eastern Orthodox, or Protestant.
>
> 3. **Latter-day Saints do not believe scripture consists of the Holy Bible alone** but have an expanded canon of scripture that includes the Book of Mormon, the Doctrine and Covenants, and the Pearl of Great Price."

In this essay, the LDS Church admits that they reject the Christian creeds that have historically defined Christianity. Joseph Smith went so far as to say in his First Vision account, recorded at **History 1:19** of their *Pearl of Great Price* LDS Scripture, that he was told to join "none" of the Christian churches of his day because **"they**

were all wrong; and the Personage who addressed me said that **all their creeds were an abomination** in his sight; that those **professors were all corrupt**."

While Mormons have often complained to us in our mission that we are "attacking" them when we expose their beliefs as un-compatible with the teachings of the Bible, we would argue that with statements like these from their Church, it is Mormonism itself that is "attacking" the churches of Christianity, and we are merely responding to their claims that teach that our Christian beliefs are "an abomination" to God.

While the Mormon Church goes on to try to justify their reasons for rejecting the historic Christian faith by claiming that Christianity apostatized (fell away from the truth) after the death of the apostles, the Bible is clear that only a few people would fall away from the faith during the apostasy. In **1 Timothy 4:1**, the Bible says, "Now the Spirit speaketh expressly, that in the latter times **some shall depart from the faith**, giving heed to seducing spirits, and doctrines of devils."[1]

Only "some," not all, will depart from the faith and this is why the Bible says in **Ephesians 3:20-21**, that God,

"...is able to do exceeding abundantly

---

[1] Unless otherwise noted, all Biblical citations are quoted from the *King James Version* of the Bible.

above all that we ask or think, according to the **power that worketh in us**, Unto him be **glory in the church** by Christ Jesus **throughout all ages**, world without end. Amen."

How could an apostate Church whose creeds are an "abomination," give "glory in the church...throughout **all** ages"? Not only does the Bible's testimony about God's preservation of His Church contradict Mormonism, but it affirms the promise of Christ who declared in **Matthew 16:18**:

"**I will build my church**; and the gates of hell **shall not prevail against it**."

Further reading in this Church essay on "Are Mormons Christian?," states:

"A third justification argued to label Latter-day Saints as non-Christian has to do with their belief in an **open scriptural canon**. For those making this argument, to be a Christian means to assent to the principle of *sola scriptura*, or the self-sufficiency of the Bible. But to claim that the Bible is the sole and final word of God—more specifically, the final written word of God—is to claim more for the Bible than it claims for itself. Nowhere does the Bible proclaim that all revelations from God would be gathered into a single volume to be forever closed and that no further scriptural revelation could be received."

While it is true that there is no specific verse in the Bible that says that God's revelation in the form of Scripture is completely closed, the Bible does say in 2 Peter 1:3:

> "According as **his divine power hath given unto us all things that *pertain* unto life and godliness**, through the knowledge of him that hath called us to glory and virtue."

If "all things" that are necessary for life and godly living were revealed to first-century Christianity, what further need do we have for more revelation from God in the form of Scripture?

By redefining Christianity to include additional works of "Scripture," Mormonism has opened the door to endless **contradictions between their Scriptures and the messages of their prophets**. Not only do their teachings disagree with the Bible (as we will examine throughout this book), but their statements disagree among themselves. For a few examples, see:

Are the Father, Son and Holy Ghost One God or Three Gods?

BOOK OF MORMON = One God	PROPHET JOSEPH SMITH = Three Gods
"And now, behold, my beloved brethren, this is the way; and there is none other way nor	"I will preach on the **plurality of Gods**... I have always declared **God** to be a distinct

name given under heaven whereby man can be saved in the kingdom of God. And now, behold, this is the doctrine of Christ, and the only and true doctrine of **the Father**, and of **the Son**, and of **the Holy Ghost, which is one God**, without end. Amen." — 2 Nephi 31:21	personage, **Jesus Christ** a **separate** and distinct personage from God the Father, and that the **Holy Ghost** was a distinct personage and a Spirit: and **these three constitute three distinct personages and three Gods**." —*Teachings of the Prophet Joseph Smith*, p. 370

Has God Always Existed, Unchangeable from all Eternity?

BOOK OF MORMON: YES	PROPHET JOSEPH SMITH: NO
"...the Lord Omnipotent who reigneth, who was, and is **from all eternity to all eternity**... For I know that God is not a partial God, neither a changeable being; but **he is unchangeable from all eternity to all eternity**." —Mosiah 3:5; 8:18	"We have imagined and supposed that **God was God from all eternity. I will refute that idea**,...he was **once a man like us**...."—*Teachings of the Prophet Joseph Smith*, pp. 345-346

Does God Dwell in the Heart of the Righteous?

BOOK OF MORMON: YES	DOCTRINE & COVENANTS: NO
"...because the Lord hath said he dwelleth not in unholy	"...the idea that **the Father and the Son dwell in a man's**

| temples, but **in the hearts of the** righteous doth he **dwell**...."—Alma 34:36 | heart is an old sectarian notion, and **is false**." -*Doctrine and Covenants* 130:3 |

Is God the Father a Personage of "Spirit" or an Exalted "Man"?

LECTURES OF FAITH and BOOK OF MORMON = "SPIRIT"	**DOCTRINE & COVENANTS AND JOSEPH SMITH, JR. = "MAN"**
"...The Father being a **personage of spirit**, glory and power: possessing all perfection and fulness..." — *Doctrine and Covenants*, 1935 edition, *Lectures Fifth of Faith*, Section V, p. 52-53 (Note: In 1921, The Lectures of Faith section was removed from *Doctrine and Covenants*.) "Holy, holy God; we believe that thou art God...that **thou art a spirit**, and that **thou wilt be a spirit forever**."—Alma 31:15, *Book of Mormon*[2]	"The **Father has a body of flesh and bones** as tangible as man's." —*Doctrine & Covenants* 130:22 "**God himself was once as we are now**, and is **an exalted Man**, and sits enthroned in yonder heavens... I say, if you were to see him to-day, you would see him like **a man in form**--like yourselves, in all the person, image, and very form as a man." —*Teachings of the Prophet Joseph Smith*, p. 345

[2] Mormons sometimes argue that because the context of this *Book of Mormon* Scripture at Alma 31 speaks of the false doctrines of the Zoramites who denied Christ (verse 16), taught a false concept of election (verse 13 and 16-18), and required their people to pray rote prayers (verse 19-20), they assume that this statement regarding God being "a spirit...forever" at verse 15 was also

Are There Two or Three Personages Governing the Universe?

LECTURES OF FAITH = TWO	JOSEPH SMITH, JR = THREE
"We shall, in this lecture speak of the Godhead: we mean the Father, Son and Holy Spirit. There are **two personages** who constitute the great, matchless, governing and supreme power over all things….They are the **Father and the Son**: The Father being a **personage of spirit**… The Son, who was in the bosom of the Father, is a personage of tabernacle…And he being the only begotten of the Father…received a fulness of the glory of the Father— possessing the same mind with the Father, which **mind is the Holy Spirit**." —*Doctrine*	"I will preach on the **plurality of Gods**…I have always declared God to be a distinct personage, Jesus Christ a separate and distinct personage from God the Father, and that the Holy Ghost was a distinct personage and a Spirit: and **these three constitute three distinct personages and three Gods**." —*Teachings of the Prophet Joseph Smith,* p. 370

another false doctrine of the Zoramites. Yet, if this doctrine was condemned as a false belief, why is there no mention in the text of the true prophet Alma and his brethren being grieved over this and trying to correct it when they grieved over other false beliefs noted at verses 24-29? Instead we see that not only is the belief that God is a "spirit" affirmed at Alma 31:15, but it is affirmed elsewhere in the *Book of Mormon* at Alma 18:24-28 and Alma 22:9-11. Thus, we maintain that Alma 31:15 is not taken out of context, nor misrepresentative of the overall teachings of the *Book of Mormon* in regard to God's Spirit nature.

and Covenants, 1935 edition, *Lectures Fifth of Faith,* Section V, p. 52-53 (Note: In 1921 edition, this *Lectures of Faith* section was removed from *Doctrine and Covenants.*)	

Should We Pray to Jesus Christ?

BOOK OF MORMON: YES	LDS CHURCH: NO
"...Jesus ...spake unto the multitude, and **commanded them that they should kneel** down again upon the earth, and also that his disciples should kneel down upon the earth. And it came to pass that when they had all knelt down upon the earth, **he commanded his disciples that they should pray.** And behold, they began to pray; and **they did pray unto Jesus,** calling him their Lord and their God." —3 Nephi 19:15-18	"Elder Bruce R. McConkie clearly explained what our relationship with each member of the Godhead should be, pointing out that some **misguided** members of the Church may '**begin to pray directly to Christ** because of some special friendship they feel has been developed' with him. **This is wrong,** said Elder McConkie. **We should pray directly to the Father...**" —*The Ensign,* June 1998, p. 59

10

Should We Worship Jesus Christ?

BOOK OF MORMON: YES	LDS CHURCH: NO
"And now behold, I say unto you that **the right way is to believe in Christ**... **wherefore ye must bow down before him, and worship him** with all your might, mind, and strength, and your whole soul; and if ye do this ye shall in nowise be cast out."—2 Nephi 25:29 "...I beheld the Son of God going forth among the children of men; and I saw **many fall down** at his feet and **worship him**."—1 Nephi 11:24 "Hosanna! Blessed be the name of the Most High God! And they did **fall down at the feet of Jesus**, and did **worship him**."—3 Nephi 11:17	"We Worship the Father... In an official interpretation of Moses 1:6, the First Presidency (Joseph F. Smith, Anthon H. Lund, And Charles W. Penrose) said: 'But the **sole object of worship, God the eternal Father,** stands supreme and alone...' Who is the **sole object of worship?**... President George Q. Cannon taught: '...We know also that our **Father in Heaven** should be the object of our worship... **He will not have any divided worship**. We are commanded to **worship Him**, and **Him only**.' (*Gospel Truth*, 1:135)" —*Come Unto Christ* —*Melchizedek Priesthood Personal Study Guide*, 1986, p. 46-47

Does God Forgive Us for Murder?

BOOK OF MORMON: YES	DOCTRINE & COVENANTS: NO
"...And I shall also thank my God, yea, my great God, that he hath granted unto us that we might repent of these things, and also that **he hath forgiven us of those our many sins and murders which we have commited**, and taken away the guilt from our hearts, through the merits of his Son."—Alma 24:10	"...And it shall come to pass, that **if any persons among you shall kill** they shall be delivered up and dealt with acccording to the laws of the land; for **remember that he hath no forgiveness**; and it shall be proved according to the laws of the land." —*Doctrine and Covenants* 42:79

Do Babies Who Die Grow in the Spirit World?

PROPHET JOSEPH SMITH: NO	JOSEPH F SMITH: YES
"But as the child dies, so shall it rise from the dead....**It will never grow: it will still be the child**, in the same precise form as it appeared before it died out of its mother's arms....Eternity is full of thrones, upon which dwell **thousands of children reigning on thrones of glory**, will not one cubit added to their stature."—Joseph Smith, 1844, *Journal of Discourses*, vol. 6, p. 10	"**All spirits are in adult form**. They were adults before their mortal existence, and **they are in adult form after death, even if they die as infants or children** (See Joseph F Smith, Gospel Doctrine, p. 455)."— *Gospel Principles*, 1992, p 290

CHAPTER ONE:

GOSPEL TOPICS ESSAYS REVEAL MORMON DIFFICULTIES

"Wherefore, confound your enemies; call upon them to meet you both in public and in private; and inasmuch as ye are faithful their shame shall be made manifest. Wherefore, let them bring forth their strong reasons against the Lord."

(Doctrine and Covenants 71:7-8)

Witnessing to Mormons Using Their Own Church History

Have you ever considered sharing your Christian faith with a Mormon friend, coworker or neighbor? Within the past few years, the basic relationship between the Mormon and the Christian, has changed forever.

For the first time in the history of the Mormon Church, authentic and realistic Mormon doctrine and history are now available to you and the Mormon people on the Gospel Topics' section of the Mormon Church's official website.

How would we know that this information was intentionally hidden from the Mormon people for so long? Because I (Lee) was a **Bishop in the Mormon Church** and a member of that faith for 32 years.

We speak from personal experience, and we desire to help guide you in bringing the Mormon people to a full knowledge of Mormon doctrine and their Church's history of deception, so that they can come to know Jesus Christ in simplicity and truth as He is taught in the Bible.

These incredibly insightful documents have been approved by the Mormon First Presidency and the Quorum of the Twelve Apostles and they now state as a fact of Mormonism, that Joseph Smith (the founder of the LDS Church whom the Mormons revere as God's Latter-day Prophet) repeatedly lied to his first wife Emma.

That he, Joseph Smith had up to **40 wives** to include **12 to 14 wives** of **other men**, whom he secretly married behind Emma's back. Many of these relationships the Mormon Church now admits included the possibility of intimate relationships.

Why does this information matter? Because it reveals the character of Joseph Smith, that he was **not** qualified to be called as one of God's latter-day prophets.

In fact, the Bible proclaims that a Bishop or Elder in a Christian church "...must be blameless, **the husband of one wife**... ." (1 Timothy 3:2, Titus 1:5-6).

If you **are a Mormon** or you have friends and loved ones involved in Mormonism, we stand with you in reaching them with the Truth of Christ as proclaimed in the Bible.

REFERENCE NOTES are from the LDS gospel Topic Essay, "Plural Marriage in Kirtland and Nauvoo," published at LDS.org. Note the following excerpts from the essay:

"**Joseph Smith and Plural Marriage**

During the era in which plural marriage was practiced, Latter-day Saints distinguished between sealings for time and eternity and sealings for eternity only. Sealings for time and eternity included commitments and relationships during this life, generally **including the possibility of sexual relations**. Eternity-only sealings indicated relationships in the next life alone. Evidence indicates that **Joseph Smith participated in both types of sealings**. The exact number of women to whom he was sealed in his lifetime is unknown because the evidence is fragmentary.[24] Some of the women who were sealed to Joseph Smith later **testified that their marriages were for time and eternity**, while others indicated that their relationships were for eternity alone.[25]"

Regarding the number of wives that Joseph Smith was married to, footnote 24 within this essay states,

"**Careful estimates put the number between 30 and 40**. See Hales, Joseph Smith's Polygamy, 2:272–73."

Regarding this fact that Joseph Smith's relationships with his plural wives included the "possibility of sexual relations," footnote 25 says,

"Despite claims that Joseph Smith fathered children within plural marriage, **genetic testing has so far been negative, though it is possible he fathered two or three children with plural wives**."

This essay also acknowledges that Joseph Smith

married teenagers as young as 14 years old when it admits,

> "The youngest was Helen Mar Kimball, daughter of Joseph's close friends Heber C. and Vilate Murray Kimball, who was sealed to Joseph **several months before her 15th birthday**."

As far as the wives that **Joseph Smith took who were "already married" to living husbands**, footnote 29 states,

> "Estimates of **the number of these sealings range from 12 to 14**. (See Todd Compton, *In Sacred Loneliness: The Plural Wives of Joseph Smith* [Salt Lake City: Signature Books, 1997], 4, 6; Hales, Joseph Smith's Polygamy, 1:253–76, 303–48.)"

On the fact that Joseph Smith's first wife **Emma only knew of four** of his 30 to 40 wives, the essay goes on to say,

> "**Joseph and Emma**...Emma approved, at least for a time, of **four** of Joseph Smith's plural marriages in Nauvoo... **But Emma likely did not know about all of Joseph's sealings**."

This is a significant admission from the LDS Church given their Scripture on the "**laws of polygamy**" in **Doctrine and Covenants 132:61** which plainly teaches that the "first" wife must give her "consent" for any additional wife and that the additional wife must be "a virgin...vowed to no other man."

> **Doctrine and Covenants 132:61**: "And again, as pertaining to the law of the priesthood—if any man espouse **a virgin**, and desire to espouse another, and **the first give her consent**, and if he espouse the second, and they are virgins, and **have vowed to no other man**, then is he justified; he cannot commit adultery for they are given unto him; for he cannot commit adultery with that that belongeth unto him and to no one else."

Evidence indicates that neither Joseph Smith nor his plural wives followed this revelation that Joseph Smith claimed he received directly from God.

In addition to Joseph Smith's failure to follow Doctrine and Covenants 132:61, this essay states that **God "commanded" Joseph Smith** to take these wives, sending an angel to threaten him with destruction if he didn't follow through. But after receiving these revelations, we see that not only did Joseph Smith hide the majority of these relationships from Emma, but he lied about them in a court of law saying on page 411 of *History of the Church,* volume 6:

> "What a thing it is for a man to be accused of committing adultery, and having seven wives, when **I can only find one**."

At the time that Joseph Smith made this statement, he had 34 wives.

This essay can be used as a powerful tool to show the deceitful character of Joseph Smith and that he was not qualified to stand as a Latter-day prophet for God's church.

Yet, in spite of the evidence that Joseph Smith was a deceiver, lying to his wife Emma and the public about his plural marriages, the LDS Church published in their 2007 manual entitled, *Teachings of Presidents of the Church Joseph Smith*, Chapter 43, page 499:

> "*Jesse N. Smith, a cousin of Joseph Smith:* '[The Prophet was] incomparably the most God-like man I ever saw. ... **I know that by nature he was incapable of lying and deceitfulness**, possessing the greatest kindness and nobility of character.' "

It's one thing to say that Joseph Smith's cousin, Jesse N. Smith, thought he was "incapable of lying," but it's quite another for the Mormon Church leaders of today to publish this statement from Jesse in an attempt to portray Joseph Smith as an honest man when he clearly was a deceiver. What does this say about the integrity of Mormon leadership today? How can anyone trust them to teach them the truth about God?

Mormon Church Gospel Topics Essays on Polygamy

HOW TO USE THE GOSPEL TOPICS ESSAYS PUBLISHED AT LDS.ORG. Regarding these essays, the Mormon Church states,

> "The purpose of these essays, which have been approved by the First Presidency and the Quorum of the Twelve Apostles, has been **to gather accurate information** from many different sources and publications and place it in the Gospel Topics section of LDS.org, where the material can more easily be accessed and **studied by Church members and other interested parties**." (*Introduction to the Essays posted at lds.org*)

We will now provide you with the a review of all thirteen "Gospel Topics Essays" that the Mormon Church has published on their website at lds.org, along with their publication dates and key statements that can be used from these essays when Christians are sharing the truth with their Mormon friends.

PLURAL MARRIAGE AND FAMILIES IN EARLY UTAH - December 16, 2013

This essay declares that polygamy (a man married to more than one woman) is not the "standard" that God has given for marriage. Within this Gospel Topics Essay, the LDS Church says,

> "The Bible and the Book of Mormon teach that the **marriage of one man to one woman is God's standard**, except at specific periods when He has declared otherwise."[1]

Footnote 1 for this paragraph reads,

> "**Jacob 2:27, 30**. For instances of plural marriage in the Bible, see Genesis 16:3; 25:1; 29:21-30; 30:3-4, 9. See also **D&C 132:34-35**."

As you can see, this footnote 1 lists the Book of Mormon reference, Jacob 2:27, 30, for God's standard being one wife for one man. But next, after trying to justify the practice by listing biblical scriptures, it gives Joseph Smith's revelation on polygamy in Doctrine and Covenants 132.

Note that while the LDS Church references the Book of Mormon Jacob 2:27 passage, which condemns marriage to more than one wife, they fail to mention verse 24 which is even stronger in its condemnation of polygamy found in the Bible. Jacob 2:24, 27-28 passage reads,

"Behold, **David and Solomon** truly had **many wives and concubines**, which thing was **abominable** before me, saith the Lord. ...Wherefore, my brethren, hear me, and hearken to the word of the Lord: For there shall not any man among you have save it be **one wife**; and **concubines he shall have none**; For I, the Lord God, delight in the chastity of women. And whoredoms are an abomination before me; thus saith the Lord of Hosts."

This essay admits that although the Mormon Church published the Manifesto in 1890 denouncing the practice of polygamy, it wasn't "strictly prohibited" until 1904. They acknowledge that, "During the years that plural marriage was publicly taught, all Latter-day Saints were expected to accept the principle as a **revelation from God**." So when the Manifesto was advocated by the Church, many Mormons,

"Believing these laws to be unjust, Latter-day Saints engaged in **civil disobedience** by **continuing to practice plural marriage and by attempting to avoid arrest**. When convicted, they paid fines and submitted to jail time. To help their husbands avoid prosecution, plural wives often separated into different households or went into hiding under assumed names, particularly when pregnant or after giving birth."

Then, the Mormon Church tries to justify their "civil disobedience" of the laws of the United States by blaming God, saying that He commanded polygamy using the very Book of Mormon passage in Jacob 2 that condemns polygamy!

> "Latter-day Saints do not understand all of **God's purposes for instituting, through His prophets, the practice of plural marriage during the 19th century**. The Book of Mormon identifies one reason for God to command it: to increase the number of children born in the gospel covenant in order to 'raise up seed unto [the Lord]' (**Jacob 2:30**)."

PLURAL MARRIAGE IN KIRTLAND AND NAUVOO - October 22, 2014

This essay confesses that Joseph Smith had between 30 and 40 wives, that he took wives as young as 14 years old, and that he married 12 to 14 wives who were already married to living husbands. This essay also acknowledges that some of Joseph Smith's plural marriages (sealings) included the "possibility" of intimate relationships and that Emma, his first wife, only knew of his marriages to "four" of his additional thirty wives. This is in direction violation of Doctrine and Covenants 132:61, where it explicitly states that the first wife must give her permission before a man is able to wed another wife. Yet, this essay claims that Joseph Smith said that an angel threatened him with death if he didn't marry these women, stating,

> "Joseph told associates that an angel appeared to him three times between 1834 and 1842 and **commanded him to proceed with plural marriage** when he hesitated to move forward. During the third and final appearance, the angel came with a drawn sword, **threatening Joseph with destruction** unless he went forward and obeyed the commandment fully."

So, in other words, Joseph Smith blamed God for his disobedience to the Mormon "laws of polygamy" given in Doctrine and Covenants 132:61.

In the Bible, we see that God never commanded polygamy and He certainly condemned any form of polyandry (marrying of over men's wives) and intermarriage with mothers and daughters.[1]

Although this essay does not mention this fact, Todd Compton's book, *In Sacred Loneliness: The Plural Wives of Joseph Smith,* (cited in this essay), provides additional details on how Joseph Smith was not only married to several wives of other men, but he was sealed to four pairs of sisters (Huntingtons, Partridges, Johnsons, Lawrences) and a mother and a

---

[1] See Leviticus 18:17-18; 20:17

daughter pair as well (Bartlett Sessions and Sylvia Sessions Lyon).[2] Regarding these "sealing" marriages, the Mormon Church claims,

> "Neither these women nor Joseph explained much about these sealings, **though several women said they were for eternity alone**.[30] Other women left no records, making it unknown whether their sealings were for time and eternity or were for eternity alone."

Then, at footnote 30, they state,

> "Polyandry, the marriage of one woman to more than one man, typically involves shared financial, residential, and sexual resources, and children are often raised communally. **There is no evidence that Joseph Smith's sealings functioned in this way**, and much evidence works against that view."

So to get around the biblical mandates against polyandry and intermarriages, the LDS Church claims, "There is no evidence that Joseph Smith's sealings functioned" in this way of polyandry. Yet, Todd Compton notes the opposite in his book, *In Sacred Loneliness,*

> "In conclusion, though it is possible that Joseph had some marriages in which there were no sexual relations, **there is no explicit or convincing evidence for**

---

[2] See pages 171, 202, 397, 475 of Todd Compton's book.

this (except, perhaps, in the cases of the older wives, judging from later Mormon polygamy). And **in a significant number of marriages, there is evidence for sexual relations**." (Todd Compton, *In Sacred Loneliness*, p. 15)

So, again the source that the Mormon Church essay is based upon, disagrees with this essay's conclusions regarding Joseph Smith's intimate marriages. But even if it could be proved that Joseph Smith avoided physical relations with the wives of other men that he "sealed" for eternity, what does this say about the Mormon belief in polygamy being practiced in heaven? The essay notes,

> "Marriage performed by priesthood authority meant that the **procreation of children and perpetuation of families** would continue into the eternities. "

So even an "eternity only" celestial marriage to nearly a dozen wives of Joseph's Smith's men, four pairs of sisters and a mother and daughter pair, goes far beyond any form of human decency and morality that could claim to be "Christian." This evidence clearly proves Joseph Smith's insatiable appetite for women in that he thought he could, at least, "seal" these wives to himself for "eternity," if not, for "time" in this life as well.

Although God may have tolerated polygamy at times, nowhere in the Bible does He ever "command" plural marriage. In fact, He strongly condemned the practice at the following verses:

> **Deuteronomy 17:15,17**: "Thou shalt in any wise set him king over thee, whom the LORD thy God shall choose: one from among thy brethren shalt thou set king over thee... **Neither shall he multiply wives to himself**, that his heart turn not away."

> **1 Timothy 3:2**: "A bishop then must be blameless, the **husband of one wife**...."

> **Titus 1:5-6**: "...ordain elders in every city, as I had appointed thee: If any be blameless, the **husband of one wife**...."

Furthermore, as the Manifesto essay (next) will cover in more detail, this essay on "Plural Marriage in Kirtland and Nauvoo," admits that Mormon leaders practiced, what is now called, "Lying for the Lord," giving a public image that is the opposite of what is being practiced, issuing "carefully worded denials," to cover-up early Mormon polygamy and polyandry:

> **"Participants in these early plural marriages pledged to keep their involvement confidential**, though they anticipated a time when the practice would be publicly acknowledged. Nevertheless, rumors spread. A few men unscrupulously used these rumors to seduce women to join them in an

unauthorized practice sometimes referred to as "spiritual wifery." When this was discovered, the men were cut off from the Church. **The rumors prompted members and leaders to issue <u>carefully worded denials</u> that denounced** spiritual wifery and **polygamy** but were **silent** about what Joseph Smith and others saw as **divinely mandated** 'celestial' plural marriage."

THE MANIFESTO AND THE END OF PLURAL MARRIAGE - October 22, 2014

This essay discusses the fact that the first Manifesto given in 1890, was used to provide a public image of monogamy for the LDS Church in order to help Utah gain acceptance into the United States. Yet, it did not stop loyal members from practicing polygamy in secret. Notice how this essay describes how early Mormon leaders practiced and encouraged "civil disobedience" to the laws of the United States, endorsing polygamy in secret, and then issued a "carefully worded" Manifesto to denounce polygamy publicly while continuing to practice it in secret:

> "Latter-day Saints sincerely desired to be loyal citizens of the United States, which they considered a divinely founded nation. But they also accepted plural marriage as a commandment from God and **believed the court was unjustly**

depriving them of their right to follow God's commands.

"Confronted with these contradictory allegiances, **Church leaders encouraged members to obey God rather than man.** Many Latter-day Saints embarked on a course of **civil disobedience** during the 1880's by continuing to live in plural marriage and to enter into new plural marriages. The federal government responded by enacting ever more punishing legislation.

"...This government opposition strengthened the Saints' resolve to resist what they deemed to be unjust laws. **Polygamous men went into hiding, sometimes for years at a time....** New plural wives had to live apart from their husbands, their confidential marriages known only to a few. **Pregnant women often chose to go into hiding,** at times in remote locales, rather than risk being subpoenaed to testify in court against their husbands. **Children lived in fear that their families would be broken up** or that they would be forced to testify against their parents. Some children went into hiding and lived under assumed names."

Once Mormon Church property began to be seized by the federal government, in accordance with the Edmunds-Tucker Act which allowed for confiscation due to the Church's refusal to end polygamy, Mormon Church President Woodruff announced the 1890 Manifesto, which was published in Doctrine and Covenants as Official Declaration 1. The essay describes it this way,

> "The Manifesto was **carefully worded** to address the immediate conflict with the U.S. government. **'We are not teaching polygamy, or plural marriage, nor permitting any person to enter into its practice**,' President Woodruff said. 'Inasmuch as laws have been enacted by Congress forbidding plural marriages, which laws have been pronounced constitutional by the court of last resort, **I hereby declare my intention to submit to those laws**, and to use my influence with the members of the Church over which I preside to have them do likewise.'"

Yet, although this first Manifesto was accepted as "authoritative and binding" by the LDS Church leadership, it did little to stop the actual practice of polygamy among the membership. This essay admits that it wasn't until 1904, when it was revealed through the testimony of Church President Joseph F. Smith, that while,

> "...the **Manifesto removed the divine command for the Church** collectively to sustain and defend plural marriage; **it**

> **had not**, up to this time, **prohibited individuals from continuing to practice** or perform plural marriage as a matter of religious conscience."

So, at the April 1904 General conference, under the leadership of Mormon Church President Joseph F. Smith, a forceful statement against polygamy was issued by the Church. Known as the Second Manifesto, this essay states,

> "The Second Manifesto was a watershed event. **For the first time**, Church members were put on notice that new plural marriages stood unapproved by God and the Church."

This statement is significant because it gives another historical example on how Mormon leaders practiced "Lying for the Lord" where they said one thing to the outside world, while practicing the opposite inside. It acknowledges that regardless of the wording of the first Manifesto being accepted as "authoritative and binding" upon the LDS Church, it wasn't until this second Manifesto was issued that the membership of the Mormon Church understood, "For the **first time**... that new plural marriages stood unapproved by God and the Church."

Essay on Mormon Violence

PEACE AND VIOLENCE AMONG 19TH-CENTURY LATTER-DAY SAINTS - May 13, 2014.

This essay declares that 19th Century Mormon leaders taught that certain sins are unforgivable unless the sinner's blood was shed to atone for their sin. They admit,

> "Drawing on biblical passages, particularly from the Old Testament, leaders taught that **some sins were so serious** that the **perpetrator's blood would have to be shed in order to receive forgiveness**. Such preaching led to increased strain between the Latter-day Saints and the relatively few non-Mormons in Utah, including federally appointed officials."

This belief, also called, "blood atonement," (see footnote 36 of the essay) led to horrific threats of violence and motivated several of the acts of vengeance performed by Mormons against their perceived enemies. Anyone who left the Mormon Church or spoke out against the Church became targets of a **"paramilitary group known as the Danites**, whose objective was to defend the community against **dissident and excommunicated Latter-day Saints**. ...Danites **intimidated** Church dissenters and other Missourians... ."

This essay goes on to explain that these Danites "were absorbed into militias largely composed of Latter-day Saints."

> **"These militias clashed with their Missouri opponents, leading to a few fatalities on both sides**. In addition, Mormon vigilantes, including many Danites, **raided two towns believed to be centers of anti-Mormon activity**, burning homes and stealing goods."

Regarding LDS Church members dealings with Indians, this essay states:

> "At times, however, Church members **clashed violently with Indians**.... At a council of Church leaders in Salt Lake City on January 31, 1850, the leader of Fort Utah reported that the Utes' actions and intentions were growing increasingly aggressive. ...In response, **Governor Young authorized a campaign against the Utes**. A series of battles in February 1850 resulted in the deaths of dozens of Utes and one Mormon. In these instances and others, some Latter-day Saints committed **excessive violence against native peoples**."

Next the essay discusses how the Mountain Meadows massacre was perpetuated against innocent civilian settlers who were traveling from Utah to California in 1857:

"At the peak of this tension, in early September 1857, a branch of the **territorial militia in southern Utah (composed entirely of Mormons)**, along with some Indians they recruited, laid siege to a wagon train of emigrants traveling from Arkansas to California. ... **Mormon militiamen planned and carried out a deliberate massacre**. They lured the emigrants from their circled wagons with a **false flag of truce** and, aided by Paiute Indians they had recruited, slaughtered them. Between the first attack and the final slaughter, the massacre destroyed the lives of **120 men, women, and children** in a valley known as Mountain Meadows. Only small children—those believed to be too young to be able to tell what had happened—were spared."

As can be seen in this essay, 19th Century Mormons were not peaceful people. They were not able to get along with any of their neighbors, whether in Ohio, Missouri, Illinois or Utah, their history of co-existence with people of other faiths and cultures is filled with accounts of lawbreaking, destruction, bloodshed and deceit.

Essays on Blacks and Women

RACE AND THE PRIESTHOOD - December 6, 2013.

This essay declares:

> "...for much of its history—from the mid-1800s until 1978—**the Church did not ordain men of black African descent to its priesthood** or allow black men or women to participate in temple endowment or sealing ordinances...

> "In 1852, President Brigham Young publicly announced that men of black African descent could no longer be ordained to the priesthood. ...Following the death of Brigham Young, **subsequent Church presidents restricted blacks from receiving the temple endowment or being married in the temple**. Over time, Church leaders and members **advanced many theories** to explain the priesthood and temple restrictions. **None of these explanations is accepted today as the official doctrine of the Church**.

> "...The justifications for this restriction **echoed the widespread ideas about racial inferiority** that had been used to argue for the legalization of black 'servitude' in the Territory of Utah. According to one view...**blacks descended**

from the same lineage as the biblical Cain, who slew his brother Abel. Those who accepted this view believed that **God's 'curse' on Cain was the mark of a dark skin**.

"...Today, the Church **disavows the theories advanced in the past that black skin is a sign of divine disfavor or curse**, or that it reflects unrighteous actions in a premortal life; that mixed-race marriages are a sin; or that blacks or people of any other race or ethnicity are inferior in any way to anyone else. Church leaders today unequivocally **condemn all racism, past and present, in any form**."

Yet, the LDS Church still upholds the racist teachings in the Book of Mormon which claims in 2 Nephi 5:21 that the Laminates were cursed with dark skin because of their sin:

"Wherefore, as they were **white**, and **exceedingly fair** and delightsome, that they might not be enticing unto my people the Lord God did cause a **skin of blackness** to come upon them."

Is this another example of a "carefully worded" statement from the LDS Church, denying its racists teachings that come straight out of their Scriptures? In addition to this racist passage in the Book of Mormon, we've identified quite a few more racially motivated statements in the Book of Mormon[1] as well as statements in another book of Mormon Scripture called, "The Pearl of Great Price." Reading these statements, we can easily see how prior Mormon leaders could have derived their teachings on racism from these verses:

> "a **blackness** came upon **all the children of Canaan**.... For the seed of Cain were **black** and had not place among them. ...king of Egypt [Pharaoh] was a descendant from the loins of Ham, and was a partaker of the **blood of the Canaanites by birth**. ... Pharaoh being of that **lineage by which he could not have the right of Priesthood**." —Moses 7:8, 22; Abraham 1:21, 27

Again, these statements are in the current editions of the Mormon Scriptures. If the Mormon leaders of today truly condemn, "**all racism, past and present, in any form,**" will they be revising their Scriptures in accordance with this new declaration, or will we discover that these statements from the LDS Church are simply "carefully worded denials" to deceive the public on the Church's true doctrines?

---

[1] See the Book of Mormon discussion later on in this book.

JOSEPH SMITH'S TEACHINGS ABOUT PRIESTHOOD, TEMPLE, AND WOMEN - October 23, 2015

This essay acknowledges that in the past, the Mormon Church allowed women to administer the priesthood blessings of healing the sick that are now reserved only for the male "Melchizedek Priesthood holders" of the church. This essay claims,

> "Joseph Smith taught that the gift of healing was a sign that would follow 'all that believe whether male or female.' During the 19th century, women frequently blessed the sick by the prayer of faith, and **many women received priesthood blessings promising that they would have the gift of healing**. ...Currently, the Church's *Handbook 2: Administering the Church* directs that 'only Melchizedek Priesthood holders may administer to the sick or afflicted.'"

Essays on Unique Mormon Beliefs

ARE MORMONS CHRISTIAN? - November 20, 2013

This essay admits that Mormonism rejects the foundational creeds that have historically defined the "Christian" faith. As such, a Mormon claiming to be a "Christian" while rejecting the foundational beliefs that make Christians who they are, is no different than a Christian claiming to be "Mormon" while rejecting the Book of Mormon and the teachings of Joseph Smith that are foundational to Mormonism.

If we allow the Mormon Church to redefine Christianity to whatever new set of beliefs they decide to accept while rejecting the historic teachings of the Christian church, that word can be applied to nearly all religions because at least most religions of today claim some sort of "belief in Jesus," that he was a "good teacher" or a "prophet" of God. Obviously, there is more to being a Christian than merely claiming belief in Jesus Christ.

BECOMING LIKE GOD - February 24, 2014

This essay discusses a foundational teaching of Mormonism that separates it from all other churches that claim to be Christian. It is the doctrine of "eternal progression" as explained by the LDS Church in this essay,

"Latter-day Saints **see all people as children of God in a full and complete sense**; they consider every person divine in origin, nature, and potential. ...Lorenzo Snow, the Church's fifth President, coined a well-known couplet: **'As man now is, God once was: As God now is, man may be.'** ...When asked about the belief in humans' divine potential, President Hinckley responded, **'Well, as God is, man may become. We believe in eternal progression. Very strongly.'** Eliza R. Snow, a Church leader and poet, rejoiced over the doctrine that we are, **in a full and absolute sense, children of God**. ...As Elder Dallin H. Oaks of the Quorum of the Twelve Apostles wrote, **'Our theology begins with heavenly parents**. Our highest aspiration is to be **like them.'** ...Divine nature and **exaltation are essential** and beloved **teachings in the Church**. ... **Latter-day Saints' doctrine of exaltation** is often similarly reduced in media to a cartoonish image of **people receiving their own planets**. ... while few Latter-day Saints would identify with caricatures of **having their own planet**, **most would agree** that the awe inspired by creation **hints at our creative potential in the eternities**."

Throughout this essay, the Mormon Church endeavors to provide support for their doctrine of men becoming gods by quoting biblical Scripture. Yet, they acknowledge,

> "The teaching that men and women have the potential to be exalted to a state of godliness **clearly expands beyond what is understood by most contemporary Christian churches**. ...These passages **can be interpreted in different ways**. Yet by **viewing them through the clarifying lens of revelations received by Joseph Smith**, Latter-day Saints see these scriptures as straightforward expressions of humanity's divine nature and potential. **Many other Christians read the same passages far more metaphorically** because they experience the Bible through the lens of doctrinal interpretations that developed over time after the period described in the New Testament."

In other words, the Mormon Church admits that its interpretations of these verses is not accepted by traditional Christianity and that one has to view these verses through the revelations of Joseph Smith in order to derive at such a distorted perspective of these verses. Later in this book, we address the specific verses that the Mormon Church quotes in this essay, and we provide strong biblical evidence contending that the LDS Church's teachings on premortal life and men exalting to godhood are unbiblical.

As far as the LDS Church's quotations of early church fathers, again they admit,

> **"What exactly the early church fathers meant when they spoke of becoming God is open to interpretation**, but it is clear that references to deification became more contested in the late Roman period and were infrequent by the medieval era."

In other words, most Christians today would disagree with the Mormon Church's interpretations of the writings of the early church fathers statements on godhood, and we would contend that if the Mormon belief in men becoming gods was taught by the first and second century Christians, why is this belief completely absent from all creedal confessions of the early Christian Church? Again, historic Christianity clearly does not support the LDS belief in the "eternal progression" of mankind.

MOTHER IN HEAVEN - October 23, 2015

This essay states, "The doctrine of a Heavenly Mother is a cherished and distinctive belief among Latter-day Saints." Yet, this essay acknowledges that there is not a single verse of Scripture or a revelation received by Joseph Smith that teaches this doctrine. They admit,

"While **there is no record of a formal revelation** to Joseph Smith **on this doctrine**, some early Latter-day Saint women recalled that he personally taught them about a Mother in Heaven. The earliest published references to the doctrine appeared shortly after Joseph Smith's death in 1844, in documents written by his close associates. The most notable expression of the idea is found in **a poem by Eliza R. Snow**, entitled 'My Father in Heaven' and now known as the hymn 'O My Father.' "

So, here we see that this foundational teaching within Mormonism is based only on a poem written by Eliza R. Snow. Yet, this teaching lies at the heart of the Mormon belief in a preexistence, which teaches that we were born spiritually to a Heavenly Father and a Heavenly Mother in a premortal world before coming to earth. It proclaims that we are here on earth to perfect ourselves in order to return to heaven with our spouses and perpetuate the family unit throughout eternity.

So this fundamental belief in a Heavenly Mother lies at the core of the unique belief system of the Mormon Church. This is why the Essays concludes with this statement, **"Our theology begins with heavenly parents**. Our highest aspiration is to **be like them.**"

Essays on the Joseph Smith Story and LDS Scriptures

FIRST VISION ACCOUNTS - November 20, 2013

This essay declares that there are **"four different accounts** of the vision" recorded by Joseph Smith and his scribes and an additional **"five accounts written by contemporaries** who heard Joseph Smith speak about the vision."

While this essay discusses some of the variations between these nine accounts and tries to provide justification for significant differences, we believe that these differences raise questions as to the credibility of the First Vision story.

For example: Did Joseph Smith see "two personages"[1], or did he see "the Lord of glory"[2] or a company of angels[3]? Did Joseph Smith learn of the apostasy of Christendom through the First Vision or was it through reading the Scriptures? Was Joseph Smith 14 years old, 15 or 16 years old? Did the angel Moroni or Nephi visit Joseph Smith in his bedroom? These are some of the discrepancies between the various accounts of the First Vision that raise doubt as to the credibility of this story. This essay admits to another fact:

---

[1] That is, God the Father and Jesus Christ, in the 1838 account.
[2] 1832 account.
[3] 1835 account.

"The earliest known account of the First Vision, the only account written in Joseph Smith's own hand, is found in a short, unpublished autobiography Joseph Smith produced **in the second half of 1832.**"

Since Joseph Smith didn't record his First Vision account until 1832, does this mean that he baptized people into the Mormon Church, which he started in 1830, without telling them about the vision? If Joseph Smith did receive such an important visitation from heaven in 1820, why couldn't he remember who he saw and why did he wait 12 years to write it down, after he had already published the Book of Mormon and converted hundreds of people into his church?

BOOK OF MORMON TRANSLATION - December 30, 2013

This essays claims that the Mormon Church officially endorses the Book of Mormon as **"the most correct of any Book on earth** & the keystone of our religion & a man would get nearer to God by abiding by its precepts than by any other Book."

This is a key statement because many changes have been made to the text of the Book of Mormon over the years and many of the teachings in the Book of Mormon actually disagree with the foundational teachings of Mormonism.

Regarding the translation of the Book of Mormon, this essay claims, "Some accounts indicate that Joseph studied the characters on the plates" while other accounts state he did not use them. The Mormon Church declares,

> "Most of the accounts speak of Joseph's use of the Urim and Thummim (either the interpreters or the seer stone), and many accounts refer to his use of a single stone. According to these accounts, **Joseph placed** either the interpreters or **the seer stone in a hat**, pressed his face into the hat to block out extraneous light, and read aloud the English words that appeared on the instrument. ...Emma ...described Joseph 'sitting with his face buried in his hat, with the stone in it, and dictating hour after hour with nothing between us.' According to Emma, **the plates 'often lay on the table without any attempt at concealment**, wrapped in a small linen table cloth.' "

For years, the LDS Church has published pictures of Joseph Smith leaning over the gold plates in an attempt to translate them. But this statement that Joseph Smith didn't even look at the gold plates when he was translating the Book of Mormon is a huge admission from the LDS Church that the gold plates may not have been used at all. However, in another account of the translation process, the essay discusses,

"The principal scribe, **Oliver Cowdery**, testified under oath in 1831 that Joseph Smith 'found with the plates, from which he translated his book, two transparent stones, resembling glass, set in silver bows. That **by looking through these, he was able to read in English, the reformed Egyptian characters, which were engraved on the plates.**' "

So did Joseph Smith translate the Book of Mormon from the text of the gold plates themselves, or did he receive the text by revelation through the seer stone? The latter story seems to provide a stronger case. This is consistent with Joseph Smith's experience as a money-digger as it was common for the person who was looking for buried treasure to use divination tools, such as stones or glass balls, to try to locate the treasure under the ground. This Essay admits in footnote 19,

"Joseph did not hide his well-known early involvement in treasure seeking. In 1838, he published responses to questions frequently asked of him. **"Was not Jo Smith a money digger," one question read. "Yes," Joseph answered**, "but it was never a very profitable job to him, as he only got fourteen dollars a month for it." [4]

---

[4] Selections from *Elders' Journal,* July 1838, 43, available at: josephsmithpapers.org. (http://www.josephsmithpapers.org/paper-summary/elders-journal-july-1838/11)

BOOK OF MORMON AND DNA STUDIES - January 31, 2014

This essay claims that the Book of Mormon "contains a record of God's dealings with... groups of people who migrated to America from the Near East..." Yet, the essay acknowledges,

> "...some people have wondered whether the migrations it describes are compatible with scientific studies of ancient America. The discussion has centered on the field of population genetics and developments in DNA science. **Some have contended that the migrations mentioned in the Book of Mormon did not occur because the majority of DNA identified** to date in modern native peoples most closely **resembles that of eastern Asian populations.** ...The evidence assembled to date suggests that **the majority of Native Americans carry largely Asian DNA.** Scientists theorize that in an era that predated Book of Mormon accounts, a relatively small group of people migrated from northeast Asia to the Americas by way of a land bridge that connected Siberia to Alaska. These people, scientists say, spread rapidly to fill North and South America and **were likely the primary ancestors of modern American Indians.**"

Being forced to reconcile with this new DNA evidence, which dispels the myth of an ancient migration from the Near East to America, this essay admits in footnote 10 that from 1981 until 2006, the Introduction to the Book of Mormon stated that the Lamanites were the **"principal ancestors** of the American Indians," while now, it has been revised to say,

> "The 2006 update to the introduction of the Book of Mormon reflects this understanding by stating that Book of Mormon peoples were **'among the ancestors** of the American Indians.'"

While the rest of this essay is dedicated to presenting reasons for not trusting the DNA evidence against the Book of Mormon migrations by claiming that the DNA "evidence is simply inconclusive." They state, "Nothing is known about the DNA of Book of Mormon peoples," and even if we could determine the specific genetic DNA markers of the Book of Mormon people, this essay states,

> "The Book of Mormon itself, however, **does not claim that the peoples it describes were either the predominant or the exclusive inhabitants of the lands they occupied**. In fact, cultural and demographic clues in its text hint at the presence of other groups."

This is a blatant lie from the Mormon Church! The Book of Mormon **does** claim that this land (America) was **"kept from the knowledge of other nations."** So how can the LDS Church say that it does not claim that its people were the "**exclusive** inhabitants of the lands they occupied" when the Book of Mormon itself says,

> **2 NEPHI 1:8**: "And behold, it is wisdom that **this land should be kept as yet from the knowledge of other nations**; for behold, many nations would overrun the land, that there would be no place for an inheritance."

> **HELAMAN 3:8**: "And it came to pass that **they did multiply and spread**, and did go forth **from the land southward to the land northward**, and did spread insomuch that they began to **cover the face of the whole earth**, from **the sea south to the sea north, from the sea west to the sea east**."

As far as not knowing anything about, "the DNA of the Book of Mormon peoples," this is simply untrue because the Book of Mormon states that these people were direct descendants of the Hebrew patriarch Joseph in the Bible. So, it is expected that a Near Eastern genetic makeup, similar to what is found in Israel today, would be present in the Native American populations here in America, yet nothing of any significance has been found.

> **ALMA 10:3**: "And Aminadi was a descendant of Nephi, who was the **son of Lehi**, who came **out of the land of Jerusalem**, who **was a descendant of**

Manasseh, who was the **son of Joseph** who was sold into Egypt by the hands of his brethren."

This, along with the fact that several artifacts mentioned in the Book of Mormon did not exist in pre-Columbian America, and the fact that archeologists have failed to uncover a single Book of Mormon coin, city, battlefield, or geographical area, provides ample evidence against the historicity of the Book of Mormon. Even this essay acknowledges this in footnote 6:

"Though there are several plausible hypotheses regarding the **geographic locations of Book of Mormon events**, the Church takes **no official position** except that the events occurred in the Americas."

The reason the LDS Church "takes no official position" on the geography of the Book of Mormon is due to the fact that nothing matches any true geographical map that we possess today. Thus, not one archaeological artifact has been uncovered in support of Book of Mormon claims. This is quite the opposite for the Bible as archeologist often start with the biblical descriptions given in the text to locate ancient cities. Yet, nothing has ever been found in support of the descriptions given in the Book of Mormon of its lands, cities and peoples.

TRANSLATION AND HISTORICITY OF THE BOOK OF ABRAHAM - July 8, 2014

In this essay, the Mormon Church acknowledges that the church officially accepts the Book of Abraham as Mormon "scripture." They also state that "fragments" of the original papyrus scrolls, which Joseph Smith claimed he translated, have been found, yet they admit that: "The relationship between those fragments and the text we have today is largely a matter of conjecture." This is due to the fact that, as they now admit in this essay:

> "**None of the characters on the papyrus fragments mentioned Abraham's name or any of the events recorded in the book of Abraham**. Mormon and non-Mormon Egyptologists agree that the characters on the fragments **do not match the translation given** in the book of Abraham, though there is not unanimity, even among non-Mormon scholars, about the proper interpretation of the vignettes on these fragments. Scholars have identified the papyrus fragments as parts of standard **funerary texts** that were deposited with mummified bodies. **These fragments date to between the third century B.C.E. and the first century C.E., long after Abraham lived**."

Did you catch what they said? The Mormon

Church officially admits that these "fragments" of the original papyrus scrolls, which Joseph Smith translated, do not even mention "Abraham's name or any of the events recorded in the book of Abraham." They were not even written during the lifetime of Abraham!

So, how could Joseph Smith claim his translations from these fragments contain the very words of Abraham when they were not even written until several hundred years after Abraham's life?

Some Mormons contend that the reason Smith's translations do not match up to Egyptologists translations is due to portions of the papyrus scrolls that were lost in the Chicago fire. Yet, these claims fall apart on two accounts:

First, Joseph Smith copied the image from the papyrus scrolls directly into his version of the Book of Abraham, along with the text of his translation. **This image is the very same image that was found in the fragments of his scrolls** that were rescued from the Chicago fire. So even if a Mormon tries to argue that the portions that Joseph Smith translated were lost, that doesn't change the fact that the image that Joseph Smith translated into his Book of Abraham does not match the true translation skilled Egyptologists give for this very same image.

And if a Mormon claims that this image in the fragment is not what Joseph Smith translated, why did Joseph Smith copy this image into his text of the Book of Abraham in the first place? The Mormon Church still prints this image in their current canonized edition of the Book of Abraham.

Secondly, the portions lost argument does not account for the unreasonable date range between the time of Abraham's life and the date these were written. This evidence alone should be enough to convince any reasonable person that Joseph Smith's claims concerning these manuscripts containing, "The writings of Abraham while he was in Egypt" are completely false. There is absolutely no way that Abraham could have written any part of these scrolls when they didn't even exist during his lifetime.

If that isn't enough to prove Joseph Smith was a fake translator, his Egyptian alphabet is another fraud, which he had started to work on before his death. The essay notes:

> "Some evidence suggests that **Joseph studied the characters on the Egyptian papyri** and attempted to learn the Egyptian language. His history reports that, in July 1835, he was **'continually engaged in translating an alphabet to the Book of Abraham**, and arrangeing a grammar of the Egyptian language as practiced by the ancients.' This 'grammar,' as it was called, consisted of columns of hieroglyphic

characters followed by English translations recorded in a large notebook by Joseph's scribe, William W. Phelps. Another manuscript, written by Joseph Smith and Oliver Cowdery, has Egyptian characters followed by explanations."

Now, this is a significant fact for the Mormon Church to admit that Joseph Smith actually tried to create a "grammar" of the language of the Egyptian scrolls he translated as the Book of Abraham. Now, let's consider this fact and compare it to an earlier statement they made in this same essay (below) and see if you can spot the lie:

> "We do know some things about the translation process. The word *translation* typically assumes an expert knowledge of multiple languages. **Joseph Smith claimed no expertise in any language**... Speaking of the translation of the Book of Mormon, the Lord said, 'You cannot write that which is sacred save it be given you from me.' The same principle can be applied to the book of Abraham. **The Lord did not require Joseph Smith to have knowledge of Egyptian**. By the gift and power of God, Joseph received knowledge about the life and teachings of Abraham."

What? "Joseph Smith claimed no expertise in any language"? And yet he created this "grammar." And what's this statement? "The Lord did not require Joseph Smith to have knowledge of Egyptian." If that was the case, why did Joseph Smith create a "grammar" of the very Egyptian language he was translating from his papyrus scroll? Does that make any sense to you? Are Mormons just supposed to accept these lies as excuses to justify Joseph Smith's fraudulent translation of the Book of Abraham?

And what does this excuse say about the Mormon view of God? That He doesn't know the Egyptian language well enough to give Joseph Smith an accurate translation? Or is this just another attempt of the Mormon Church to place Joseph Smith's frauds at Jesus' feet claiming, God gave Joseph Smith this translation. Are you kidding me? Blaming these lies on God should be disgraceful for any true follower of Jesus Christ to accept!

Now regarding the Joseph Smith's grammar, the Mormon Church acknowledges,

> "The relationship of these documents to the book of Abraham is not fully understood. **Neither the rules nor the translations in the grammar book correspond to those recognized by Egyptologists today**. Whatever the role of the grammar book, it appears that Joseph Smith began translating portions of the book of Abraham almost immediately after the purchase of the

papyri. Phelps apparently viewed Joseph Smith as **uniquely capable of understanding the Egyptian characters**: 'As no one could translate these writings,' he told his wife, 'they were presented to President Smith. He soon knew what they were.'"

Wow! Here again, we get a glimpse as to Joseph Smith's claim to be an expert on the Egyptian language. If he wasn't behaving in such a way as to deceive his own scribe, William W. Phelps, as to his knowledge of the Egyptian language, why didn't he correct Phelps' misunderstanding of his translation abilities?

Finally, the essay admits that without their Book of Abraham, many of their fundamental teachings, which most Christians reject, such as their views about the preexistence of humanity and Jesus and Lucifer being spirit-brothers, would not exist. So, if this book is a fraud, these teachings must be discarded as well. The essay states this:

> "**The book of Abraham clarifies several teachings that are obscure in the Bible**. Life did not begin at birth, as is commonly believed. **Prior to coming to earth, individuals existed as spirits**. In a vision, Abraham saw that one of the spirits was "like unto God." **This divine being, Jesus Christ**, **led other spirits** in **organizing** the earth out of "materials" or

preexisting matter, not ex nihilo or out of nothing....**Nowhere in the Bible is the purpose and potential of earth life stated so clearly as in the book of Abraham**."

Again, these unbiblical teachings of the Book of Abraham must be rejected by true Christianity.

CHAPTER TWO:

JOSEPH SMITH AND HIS TRANSLATIONS

"If a faith will not bear to be investigated; if its preachers and professors are afraid to have it examined, their foundation must be very weak."

— George A. Smith (Apostle) (Journal of Discourses, Vol. 14, 1871, p. 216)

Did Joseph Smith See God the Father?

Mormonism stands or falls on the story of its founder, Joseph Smith. Did God the Father and Jesus Christ really appear to Joseph Smith telling him that all the churches and creeds of Christianity are wrong?

Many inconsistencies in the story of Joseph Smith's First Vision led us to question the historical validity of his claims. If God did appear to Joseph Smith in 1820, why did he wait **12 years** before he even wrote it down in his 1832 Diary? Did Joseph Smith learn about the apostasy through reading the Scriptures as he says in his Diary account or did God reveal it to him directly in the vision as he claimed later? And who did Joseph Smith see? Was it the Father and the Son, the Lord Jesus alone, or was it a company of angels?

Joseph Smith couldn't even keep his own angel story straight. The official account published by the Mormon Church teaches that Joseph Smith was visited by the angel **Moroni** who buried the Gold Plates of the Book of Mormon. But in Joseph Smith's handwritten version of that account, he wrote that the angel **Nephi** visited him.

Yet, the angel Nephi could not have shown Smith the location of the plates because according to the Book of Mormon history, he died several centuries before the plates were even written!

Not only do the historical records of Joseph Smith's story raise doubt as to the credibility of his claims, but biblical Scripture contradicts his claim to see God when it teaches that no man has ever seen God at anytime (John 1:18).

By attacking Christianity in his First vision when he claims that all the Christian creeds are an abomination to God (Joseph Smith—History 1:19), Mormonism distorts the gospel and cannot be considered Christian.

REFERENCE NOTES:

JOSEPH SMITH'S HANDWRITTEN ACCOUNT
http://www.josephsmithpapers.org/paper-summary/history-circa-1841-draft-draft-3/6

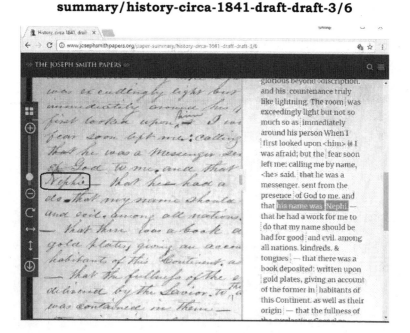

Are Feelings the Proper Way to Determine Truth?

How do we know if a prophet has truly been sent from God? Was Marshall Applewhite, the Heaven's Gate cult prophet, speaking from God when he encouraged his followers to commit suicide to join the Hale–Bopp Comet in 1997? Or what about the Branch Davidian cult prophet David Koresh, whose followers perished in the Waco Texas fire in 1993?

There is no lack of false prophets who have proclaimed revelations supposedly from God but that have turned out destructive in the lives of their followers. So how can we test if Joseph Smith, the founder of Mormonism, was a true prophet of God?

When I was considering joining the LDS Church, the missionaries encouraged me to "pray" about the Book of Mormon to see if it was true. They told me that if I received a special feeling, this proved that Mormonism was true.

But are feelings the proper way to test the truth about a religion or prophet? I'm sure all of the people who died in these other cults had "feelings" that their prophets were from God, but obviously those feelings were given to them by false spirits. The Bible says, "...believe not every spirit, but **try** (or test) the spirits whether they are of God: because many false prophets are gone out into the world" (1 John 4:1).

So how can we test the spirit of Mormonism and the claims of the prophet Joseph Smith? The Bible says, "To the law and to the testimony: **if they speak not according to this word, *it is* because *there is* no light in them.**" (Isaiah 8:20)

There's nothing wrong in praying for truth (John 8:32), but the answer to truth is never based on feelings. Scripture tells us "the heart is deceitful" and cannot be trusted (Jeremiah 17:9). Truth is based upon facts and the facts prove that the teachings of Joseph Smith do not agree with the "law" and the "testimony" of biblical prophets. So Joseph Smith cannot be considered a prophet of God. Consider this chart:

JOSEPH SMITH VS. THE BIBLE:

JOSEPH SMITH	THE BIBLE
God was once a man and men can become gods (The King Follett discourse).	**God** is not an exalted man (Hosea 11:9). He has always been God (Psalm 90:2).
Jesus is the "spirit brother" of Lucifer who competed with him to become Savior of the World (Moses 4, Book of Abraham 3, and Church Manual, *Gospel Principles*, Chapter 3).	**Jesus** is the eternal God, the Creator of all things, including the angels and Lucifer (John 1:1-3; Colossians 1:15-17, 2:9). He never competed with Satan for the role of Savior.
Bible is not accurate (8th Article of Faith, 1 Nephi 13:26-28).	**Bible** is accurately preserved. Nothing is lost (Matthew 24:35).

Did Joseph Smith Lead the Church Astray?

When I (Kathy) was growing up in Mormonism, I was taught that God would never allow a prophet to lead the church astray.[1]

Yet, recent statements from the Mormon Church seem to contract this teaching when they say, "... **we must be worthy** and **receive inspiration** from the Holy Ghost **in order to know** when the Brethren speak by the power of the Holy Ghost..." The Church manual, *Teachings of the Living Prophets,* then says, "In a way, this completely **shifts the responsibility from them to us** to determine when they so speak" by the Holy Ghost."[2] So, if it's up to us, individuals, to determine if a prophet is speaking from God, then what's the point of having a living prophet leading the Church in the first place?

In the Bible, God warns that if a prophet "...shall presume to speak a word in my name, **which I have not commanded him to speak**, ...even **that prophet shall die**. ... When a prophet speaketh in the name of the LORD, **if the thing follow not, nor come to pass**, that is the thing which the LORD hath not spoken...."[3] So the Bible is clear. There is no room for God's

---

[1] See statements of President Wilford Woodruff quoted in *Gospel Principles, Chapter 9: Prophets of God.*

[2] See *Teachings of the Living Prophets Student Manual,* Chapter 6: General Conference, p. 73.

[3] Deuteronomy 18:20-22

prophets to give revelations that are not from Him.

So, did Joseph Smith give false revelations?

History shows that he did. *Doctrine and Covenants* records two temple prophecies that failed when Mormons were driven out of Missouri (See Doctrine and Covenants Sections 84 and 115). And in *Doctrine and Covenants* Section 103, Joseph Smith received a revelation to form a group of men, called Zion's Camp, to reclaim their Missouri land. But the mission failed miserably with men dying of sickness along the way.

Reading these false prophecies, which never came to pass, we can see that history proves Joseph Smith was not a true prophet sent from God, so Mormonism cannot be true.

ADDITIONAL THOUGHTS:

Some Mormons argue that the reason the Zion's Camp prophecy failed was due to some type of unfaithfulness among the LDS saints as the revelation says, "All victory and glory is brought to pass unto you through your diligence, faithfulness, and prayers of faith." (D&C 103:36) Yet, historical documents do not reveal a single way in which they were unfaithful. In every aspect, they carried out the demands perfectly. So claiming unfaithfulness on the part of the saints doesn't justify this false prophecy.

Did Joseph Smith Change God's Revelations?

Did Joseph Smith change the very revelations that he claimed God gave him? The Mormon Scripture called, *Doctrine and Covenants,* records revelations Joseph Smith received **directly** from God. Joseph Smith originally published these revelations in a book called, *The Book of Commandments,* in 1833. Later, these very same revelations were republished as the *Doctrine and Covenants* in 1835. While there is no indication that these revelations were ever redelivered to Joseph Smith by God, he took the liberty to make significant changes to these revelations, when they were republished, that included the deletion and addition of several words, sentences and paragraphs.

One significant change that Joseph Smith made, occurs at **Doctrine and Covenants section 27** where Joseph Smith claims to receive the priesthood "keys of authority" that forms the very basis of the Mormon Melchizedek Priesthood leadership system. Yet, this whole section of Scripture is completely missing in the original version published in chapter 28 of the *Book of Commandments.*

Another significant change is found in the *Book of Commandments* chapter 4 where God tells Joseph Smith that after translating the Book of Mormon, He would "grant him **no other gift**" to translate. But later when Joseph Smith translated the *Book of Abraham*, he changed this revelation to say, "this is the **first gift** that I bestowed upon you" in ***Doctrine and Covenants*, Section 5 verse 4**.

Not only did Joseph Smith change *Doctrine and Covenants*, he corrected the *Book of Mormon* in later editions as well, changing phrases like **1 Nephi 13:40** where, "the Lamb of God is the eternal Father" is changed to "the **Son of the** eternal Father" and **Mosiah 21:28** where "King **Benjamin**" is changed to "King **Mosiah**." By changing revelations he claimed were from God, Joseph Smith proved he was a charlatan and not a true prophet of God.

REFERENCE NOTES
Book Of Commandments Section 4:

should not show them except I command him, and he has no power over them except I grant it unto him; and he has a gift to translate the book, and I have commanded him that he shall pretend to no other gift, for I will grant him no other gift. 3 And verily I say unto you, that wo shall come unto the inhabitants of the earth, if they will not hearken unto my words, for, behold, if they will not

http://www.josephsmithpapers.org/paper-summary/book-of-commandments-1833/14

Compared With Doctrine & Covenants 5:4:

4 And you have a **gift to translate** the plates; and this is the **first gift** that I bestowed upon you; and I have commanded that you should **pretend to no other gift until my purpose is fulfilled** in this; for I will grant unto you no **other gift until it is finished**.

CHANGES BETWEEN THE
Book of Commandments Chapter 4 and
Doctrine and Covenants Section 5

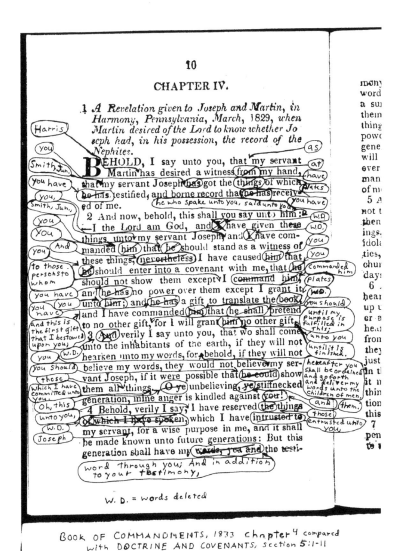

Book of Commandments Chapter 28 and Doctrine and Covenants Section 27

Moroni, whom I have sent unto you to reveal the Book of Mormon, containing the fulness of my everlasting gospel, to whom I have committed the keys of the record of the stick of Ephraim; And also with Elias, to whom I have committed the keys of bringing to pass the restoration of all things spoken by the mouth of all the holy prophets since the world began, concerning the last days; And also John the son of Zacharias, which Zacharias he (Elias) visited and gave promise that he should have a son, and his name should be John, and he should be filled with the spirit of Elias; which John I have sent unto you, my servant, Joseph Smith, Jun., and Oliver Cowdery, to ordain you unto the first priesthood which you have received, that you might be called and ordained even as Aaron; And also Elijah, unto whom I have committed the keys of the power of turning the hearts of the fathers to the children, and the hearts of the children to the fathers, that the whole earth may not be smitten with a curse; And also with Joseph and Jacob and Isaac, and Abraham, your fathers, by whom the promises remain; And also with Michael, or Adam, the father of all, the prince of all, the ancient of days; And also with Peter, and James, and John, whom I have sent unto you, by whom I have ordained you and confirmed you to be apostles, and especial witnesses of my name, and bear the keys of your ministry and of the same things which I revealed unto them; Unto whom I have committed the keys of my kingdom, and a dispensation of the gospel for the last times; and for the fulness of times, in the which I will gather together in one all things, both which are in heaven, and which are on earth; And also with

CHAPTER XXVIII.

1 *A Commandment to the church of Christ, given in Harmony, Pennsylvania, September 4, 1830.*

LISTEN to the voice of Jesus Christ, your Lord, your God and your Redeemer, whose word is quick and powerful.

2 For behold I say unto you, that it mattereth not what ye shall eat, or what ye shall drink, when ye partake of the sacrament, if it so be that ye do it with an eye single to my glory;

3 Remembering unto the Father my body which was laid down for you, and my blood which was shed for the remission of your sins:

4 Wherefore a commandment I give unto you, that you shall not purchase wine, neither strong drink of your enemies:

5 Wherefore you shall partake of none, except it is made new among you, yea, in this my Father's kingdom which shall be built up on the earth.

6 Behold this is wisdom in me, wherefore marvel not, for the hour cometh that I will drink of the fruit of the vine with you, on the earth, and with all those whom my Father hath given me out of the world:

7 Wherefore lift up your hearts and rejoice, and gird up your loins, and be faithful until I come:— (even so.) Amen.

and ye shall be caught up, that where I am ye shall be also.

and take upon you my whole armor, that ye may be able to withstand the evil day, having done all, that ye may be able to stand. Stand, therefore, having your loins girt about with truth, having on the breastplate of righteousness, and your feet shod with the preparation of the gospel of peace, which I have sent mine angels to commit unto you; Taking the shield of faith wherewith ye shall be able to quench all the fiery darts of the wicked; And take the helmet of salvation, and the sword of my Spirit, which I will pour out upon you, and my word which I reveal unto you, and be agreed as touching all things whatsoever ye ask of me,

BOOK OF COMMANDMENTS chapter 28 compared with DOCTRINE AND COVENANTS Section 27

Is Black Skin a Curse from God?

Have you ever **read** the Book of Mormon? Did you know that the Book of Mormon, that is in print today, and given away free by the Mormon Missionaries, is the **most racist** set of Scriptures of any religion in the **world**?

Hundreds of thousands of Mormons have never **really** read the Book of Mormon. Which is a bit **strange**, because the Book of Mormon is the very foundation of the Mormon Faith. The Book of Mormon clearly states, several times, that **black skin** is a curse from God. Yet the Bible teaches in John 3:16 that God so loved the world...not just the people with white skin.

The Book of Mormon tells of a **violent** struggle between two groups of people somewhere in South, Central or North America. In the Book of Mormon story, the good, hard-working people are **white** and the violent and lazy group is **black**.

The Book of Mormon, 2 Nephi 30:6, claims that if the **bad black** people repent, then they too will become white like the good people. The current Book of Mormon warns both groups of people that they should not "**mix**" their seed between the **blacks** and **whites** or God will curse them.

As former members of the Mormon Church, we know very well that **most Mormons are not racist.** Yet, in over 180 years of changing many other parts of the Book of Mormon, the Mormon

Leadership still prints and reprints **35 remarkably racist statements** found in the current Book of Mormon. Past Mormon Doctrine taught that the **black race** was permitted to come through the Great Flood and remain on earth to represent **Satan**.[1]

Lee and I have worked very closely with several Black Communities around the world, and we are just **astonished**, that **any** person of Color would join the Mormon Church.

We are equally amazed and stunned that **any white Mormon** would continue to endorse, admire or much less **teach** from the Book of Mormon. The Book of Mormon is **wrong**, Black Skin is not now and **never was** a curse from God. The plague of Racism and Bigotry may be promoted within the Book of Mormon, but it is **not** found in the Bible.

ADDITIONAL THOUGHTS:

The 1830 edition and most early editions of the Book of Mormon stated in **2 Nephi 30:6** that the Nephites would become "a **white** and delightsome people" but in the 1981 edition, the Mormon Church changed this verse to read "a **pure** and delightsome people." However, all the other references to black skin being a curse are still in the current edition of the Book of Mormon.

---

[1] See John Taylor, *Journal of Discourses, vol. 22,* pp. 303-304.

MORE INFORMATION ON MORMON RACISM:

Reference to the Statement from Mormonism above about the Blacks Representing Satan:

Journal of Discourses, vol. 22, pages 303-304:

"For although they were destroyed in the body, yet when Jesus came and ...preached to the spirits in prison that were disobedient in the days of Noah. And then the devil put on a long face and said, I imagined I had got rid of these fellows; but they are going to have a chance yet that I did not think of. And **after the flood we are told that the curse that had been pronounced upon Cain was continued through Ham's wife**, as he had married a wife of that seed. And why did it pass through the flood? **Because it was necessary that <u>the devil should have a representation upon the earth as well as God;</u>** and that man should be a free agent to act for himself, and that all men might have the opportunity of receiving or rejecting the truth, and be governed by it or not according to their wishes and abide the result; and that those who would be able to maintain correct principles under all circumstances, might be able to associate with the Gods in the eternal worlds. It is the same eternal programme. God knew it and Adam knew it." – Discourse by President John Taylor, Delivered at Provo on August 28th, 1881.

Book of Mormon Teachings on Black Skin:

1 Nephi 11:13 – The Virgin Mary was fair and **WHITE** like the good people.

1 Nephi 12:23 – Wicked people became **DARK** because of the curse from God.

1 Nephi 13:15 – Good people were all **WHITE** as a gift from God.

2 Nephi 5:21 – God cursed all bad people with **BLACK** skin.

Jacob 3:5, 8-9 – Bad **BLACK** people can become good and then become **WHITE**.

Alma 3:6-19 – Bad **BLACK** people should <u>not</u> mix with good **WHITE** people, it is a sin.

3 Nephi 2:14-16 – If bad **BLACK** people became good, they then can become **WHITE**.

3 Nephi 19:25, 30 – All good people and <u>Jesus</u> are **WHITE**.

Mormon 5:15 – All bad people to be scattered and become **BLACK**.

The God of the Bible is NOT Racist. He Accepts All People: Romans 2:11, John 3:16, Acts 10:34, Galatians 3:28

Some Mormons argue that racism against the blacks is taught in the Bible where God curses Cain with a mark (Genesis 4:15-16), but nowhere is dark skin implied as a curse, nor is this curse of Cain ever passed down to his children. Likewise, the curse on Ham and Canaan (Genesis 9-10) is never said to be dark skin.

Where Did the Book of Mormon Come From?

Joseph Smith said he translated the Book of Mormon from gold plates he found in New York. He said these plates contained the records of ancient inhabitants of America who migrated from Israel in about 600 B.C.

Yet, not a single **coin**, **city**, or **battle field** mentioned in the Book of Mormon has ever been identified in any archeological dig in America. Animals mentioned in the Book of Mormon such as the **cow**, **horse**, **ox**, **ass**, and **goat** as well as commodities such as **wheat**, **barley**, **silk**, **steel**, **brass** and the **compass** were either unknown in Book of Mormon times or did not exist in Pre-Columbian America. **DNA evidence** for a Jewish migration to America is also lacking.

So where did the Book of Mormon come from? We believe that Joseph Smith borrowed from a number of contemporary books of his day when he wrote the Book of Mormon. Not only did he plagiarize whole chapters of the Bible, he borrowed names, phrases and stories from three other books: *The Late War Between the United States and Great Britain, The First Book of Napoleon,* and *The View of the Hebrews* by Ethan Smith.

I used to think that the idea of the lost 10 tribes of Israel migrating to America and the story of Samuel the Lamanite preaching over the wall of a city while stones were thrown at him were stories unique to the Book of Mormon. But these ideas and similar stories are found in the fictional book called *The View of the Hebrews* published by Ethan Smith in 1825.

So the evidence proves that the Book of Mormon is not a true historical record, nor is its message compatible with God's Word, the Bible, so Mormonism cannot be a religion from God.

ADDITIONAL THOUGHTS:

While Joseph Smith drew from the ideas in these books when he was creating his Book of Mormon stories, no single story retold in the Book of Mormon is reiterated exactly as it was in these books. For example, the story of Samuel, the Lamanite Prophet, given in Heleman 13-16 of the Book of Mormon, is similar to the story of Jesus, son of Ananus, found on page 20 of the *View of Hebrews,* who climbed upon the city wall to preach "Wo, wo to this city" while stones were thrown at him. While the character in the *View of the Hebrews* died from his wounds, Samuel the Lamanite was protected from the stones and survived.

The fact that differences such as these exist is not surprising as Joseph Smith could not have sold his book if he didn't change some of the details for his audience who were familiar with these books. So, differences do not discount the evidence he likely drew ideas from these sources.

Is the Book of Mormon Against Mormonism?

Have you ever been challenged by a Mormon friend or neighbor to read and pray about the Book of Mormon to see if it is true? Did you know the Book of Mormon which Joseph Smith claimed is the "most correct of any book of earth" and the "keystone" of the Mormon religion (See Introduction to the Book of Mormon) **does not contain any of the unique doctrines of Mormonism?**

Examples of **key Mormon doctrines that are NOT taught in the Book of Mormon** are:

1.) The Spirit-World, Pre-existence, or
   Premortal life (the Mormon idea that mankind existed as spirits before coming to earth).

Not in the Book of Mormon.

2.) The 3 Kingdoms of Heaven: The Telestial
   Kingdom, the Terrestrial Kingdom and the Celestial Kingdom.

Not in the Book of Mormon.

3.) The Plan of Salvation: Here is a key
   doctrine of the Mormon Church. They claim to know where you came from, why you are here and where you are going. That is not in the Book of Mormon.

Not in the Book of Mormon.

3.) Marriage for time an eternity.

<u>Not</u> in the Book of Mormon.

4.) Baptism for the dead, a second chance after death in the Spirit World.

<u>Not</u> in the Book of Mormon. In fact it teaches the opposite at **Alma 34:32-35** when it claims that this life is the only life we have to repent and that there is no second chance after you die.

5.) God was once a man and men can become gods.

<u>Not</u> in the Book of Mormon. It teaches the opposite at **Moroni 8:18** where it says, "For I know that God is not a partial God, neither a changeable being; but he is **unchangeable from all eternity to all eternity**."

6.) The Father, the Son and Holy Ghost are three separate gods.

<u>Not</u> in the Book of Mormon. Here again it teaches clearly the Trinity at **2 Nephi 31:21**: "...behold, this is the doctrine of Christ, and the only and true doctrine of the **Father**, and of the **Son**, and of the **Holy Ghost**, **which is one God**, without end. Amen."

In conclusion, if you get the character of God wrong, you get everything wrong.

Did Joseph Smith Translate Fraudulent Plates?

In *History of the Church,* volume 5, page 372, we read about six small bell-shaped plates, unearthed in Kinderhook, Illinois with inscriptions on them. When these plates were presented to Joseph Smith in 1843, he said, "**I have translated a portion of them**, and find **they contain the history** of the person with whom they were found. He was a descendant of Ham, through the loins of Pharaoh, king of Egypt, and that he received his kingdom from the Ruler of heaven and earth."

Later, two individuals, W.P. Harris and Wilbur Fugate, admitted their involvement in the conspiracy of forging these bogus plates to test Joseph Smith's translation abilities. Then, in the August 1981 edition of the LDS magazine titled the *Ensign,* the Mormon Church admitted that recent metallurgy performed on one of the plates shows that the "**Kinderhook Plates Brought to Joseph Smith Appear to Be a Nineteenth-Century Hoax**."

While Joseph Smith did not translate more than this, no one can deny that he was impressed with them and thought they were authentic. Although this fact should raise doubt as to Joseph Smith's translation abilities, even more troubling is the *Book of Abraham* that Joseph Smith translated from fragments of an Egyptian burial text.

Regarding this Mormon Scripture from the *Pearl of Great Price*, the LDS Church now admits, "Mormon and non-Mormon Egyptologists agree that the characters on the fragments **do not match** the translation given in the book of Abraham." So how can we trust Joseph Smith when the evidence proves he was a charlatan and not a prophet of God?

ADDITIONAL THOUGHTS:

Mormons often try to excuse the evidence against the Book of Abraham by claiming that we do not possess the portions of the papyrus scrolls which Joseph Smith translated into his Book of Abraham. Yet, as pointed out in our discussion of the Mormon Church essay in chapter one of this book, this argument fails on the fact that Joseph Smith copied the image of the papyrus fragments into his translation of the Book of Abraham, and this is the very same image identified on the fragments of the papyrus scrolls discovered.

The Church now admits that Joseph Smith's translation of this image does not match the translation given by Egyptologists. Likewise, the date these manuscripts were written proves that they were not in existence during Abraham's lifetime. So, even if we could find the missing fragments, these couldn't contain Abraham's words as translated by Joseph Smith.

CHAPTER THREE:

THE MORMON VIEW OF GOD AND MAN

"I say to the whole world, receive the truth, no matter who presents it to you. Take up the Bible, compare the religion of the Latter-day Saints with it, and see if it will stand the test."

—Brigham Young (2nd Prophet) (Journal of Discourses, Vol. 16, 1873, p. 46)

Was God Once a Man?

As a Mormon, I (Kathy) used to wonder, "Why would anyone feel the need to question if **Mormons** are Christian? Even the name of the Church reflects the Mormon belief in Jesus Christ." I was proud to be called a member of "The Church of **Jesus Christ** of Latter-day Saints."

It is true that the **name** of Jesus Christ **is** there, **but** the Mormons believe in a **completely different** Jesus Christ than the entire Christian world believes in. To the Mormon, Jesus Christ is our Elder Brother and in Mormon Scripture Jesus Christ is truly and literally the **Son of God**. "But, which God?," asked Lee.

Kathy replied, "What do you mean when you say, '**Which God**' "?

"Well, just ask any Mormon, 'Is it true that you believe that God was once just a man like us? You believe this **unknown man** progressed to become a God, in-fact the God of our world?' "

Doesn't one of the Mormon Gospel Topics Essays titled, "**Becoming Like God**," quote the Mormon Prophet Lorenzo Snow, as stating, "**As man now is, God once was: As God now is, man may be?**" It is the very **Nature and Character of God** that sets Mormonism apart from the Christians.

The God of the Bible says at **Malachi 3:6**, "For I am the Lord. **I change not.**" God also tells us in **Isaiah 43:10**, "**...before me there was no God formed, neither shall there be after me.**" Mormonism clearly does not agree with God's Word in the Bible. He never progressed from a mortal man to become a God. He has always been God (**Psalm 90:2**). So, I do not see how the Mormon Church can claim that they are Christian when they have changed the very nature and character of God as spoken of by God Himself in the Bible.

ADDITIONAL THOUGHTS:

If the Mormon teaching were true that God was once a man "like us," **wouldn't that make him once a sinner "like us"?** Since Jesus was "without sin," (Hebrew 4:15), how could He do something His Father couldn't do? Mormonism perverts the nature of God and falls under the **condemnation of Romans 1:22-23,** which teaches that fools "changed the glory of the uncorruptible God **into an image made like to corruptible man.**"

The Bible is clear that not only were no gods formed "before" or "after" Him (Isaiah 43:10). He alone is the "...Alpha and Omega, the beginning and the end, the **first** and the **last**" God, the **"Almighty"** at **Revelation 22:13** and **Revelation 1:8.** Being the "**Almighty**" God, He can have no equal.

Are We in the Process of Becoming Gods?

Quite often when we speak about how Mormons aren't Christians because they believe that they can become gods, people say, "I know a doctor, a dentist, a lawyer who is a Mormon. There is no way these smart people believe this about God."

While it is true that not every Mormon knows these deeper doctrines of Mormonism, that doesn't change the fact that this is still the official teaching of the Mormon Church. How do Lee and I know this to be true? Because **I** (Kathy) was a **Mormon for almost 50 years**.

We know, because **I** (Lee) was an **Active Mormon for 32 years and Mormon Bishop.** We were taught that not only was our **God just an exalted man**, but that all men and women will have the opportunity to become gods and goddesses of their own worlds. This is still a **core** belief of Mormonism today. In-fact, the Headquarters of the Mormon Church has issued an Official statement in their "**Becoming Like God**" gospel Topic Essay on their church website that describes how **you** can become a god.

Now ask, "How can Mormons be considered Christian when they believe they can become gods of their own worlds? Wouldn't that make multiple gods?"

In **Isaiah 44:6**, God says, "**I am the first, and I am the last**; and **beside me there is no God.**"

In **Isaiah 46:9** the LORD says, "I *am* God, and there is none else; *I am* God, and there is **none like me**."

Paul warns the Galatians in chapter one verses seven and nine, "Evidently some people are throwing you into confusion and are trying to **pervert the gospel of Christ**. ... If anybody is preaching to you **a gospel other than what you accepted**, let them be under God's curse!" (NIV) With the teaching that you can becoming a god of your own world, Mormonism completely perverts the gospel of Christ and cannot be considered Christian.

ADDITIONAL THOUGHTS:

Another verse that supports the biblical Christian belief that the God of the Bible has no gods formed before Him is **Hebrews 6:10** which states, "For when God made promise to Abraham, **because he could swear by no greater, he sware by himself**." If God, our Father, was once a man who progressed to godhood with a father who existed and had progressed to godhood before Him, this verse would not make any sense because God could simply swear by His Father. But here, the Bible clearly refutes this false teaching by stating that God our Father could not swear by anyone greater than Himself.

Is God's Image Human?

If you're a Mormon who considers yourself to be a Christian, I want you to **seriously consider** what you are teaching your children about God. Growing up in Mormonism, I (Kathy) was taught that God is an exalted man like us, and that someday, all men and women on this earth will have the opportunity to become gods and goddesses of their own worlds. But where does this non-Christian doctrine come from?

The Mormon Church claims in their gospel Topic Essay on "Becoming like God" that this doctrine is taught in the first chapter of Genesis where "God said, **Let us make man** in **our** image, after **our likeness**" (**Genesis 1:26**). But every Mormon needs to consider the irrationality of that argument. Who was the "**us**" that God was talking to when He said, "Let **us make man** in **our image**, after **our likeness**."? Was it not the Godhead, which is comprised of the Father, the Son (Jesus Christ), and the Holy Ghost? Is there a single Mormon today who believes that the Holy Ghost has a physical human body?

No. Mormons don't believe the Holy Ghost has a human body.

And what about Jesus Christ? Did He possess a physical human body at that time when God created Adam and Eve?

No. Not a single Mormon believes that Jesus had a physical human body before He was born on the earth.

So how can the Mormon Church claim that the "image" and "likeness" of God that the Godhead gave to Adam and Eve at creation was a physical human body when neither the Son nor the Holy Ghost possessed a human body at that time? Not only does Genesis **not** support the Mormon belief in "becoming like God" it argues against this very doctrine at Genesis 3, where we read that it was Satan's idea that by eating the forbidden fruit, men would become "like" God. Mormonism distorts the very character of God Himself, and if you get the character of God wrong, you get everything wrong.

ADDITIONAL THOUGHTS:

When **God is described in human terms**, this does not mean God is human any more than God being described with "wings" and "feathers" makes Him a bird (**Psalm 91:4**). Rather these physical descriptions of God, also called "anthropomorphisms," are used to help our finite minds relate to this transcendent, infinite and eternal God. **Colossians 3:10** shows that the image God created us in is a **spiritual image** and not a physical one when it says, "...put on the **new man**, which is renewed in **knowledge** after **the image of him that created him**." In the same way, when **2 Peter 1:4** speaks of us partaking of the "**divine nature**," it is speaking of our **spiritual image** that is renewed in holiness upon acceptance of Christ.

Did Jesus Teach Men Can Become Gods?

Did Jesus teach the Mormon doctrine that men can become "Gods" of their own universe?

In the Mormon Church gospel Topic Essay on "Becoming like God" they claim that Jesus taught that humans are in the process of becoming gods when he quoted **Psalm 82:6** at John 10:34 saying, "Is it not written in your law, I said, **Ye are gods?**"

As with most Scriptures the Mormon Church quotes to support their blasphemous doctrine of men becoming gods, they fail to consider the context of these statements. Let's start with Psalm 82, which forms the bases of Jesus' reference about being "gods" at John 10:34.

Here the Psalmist says, "How long will ye **judge unjustly**, and accept the persons of the wicked? ...I have said, **Ye are gods**; and all of you are children of the most High. **But ye shall die like men**, and fall like one of the princes."

Rather than complimenting these wicked judges for their attempt to be "gods," the true God of the Bible is actually **mocking** them because these wicked judges were convicting the innocent while acquitting the guilty. In other words, these wicked judges were doing **exactly** what the Pharisees were doing to Jesus when they picked up stones to condemn Jesus, the true God, to death.

In Psalms 82, it's as if the true God is saying to

these wicked judges, "You think you're gods but you will die like the men that you truly are!"

And in quoting Psalms 82 at John 10, Jesus was reminding the Pharisees of the serious consequences of their judgment of Him, stating that what these Pharisees thought they were in trying to act as gods, when He was in reality, the one true God.

In reducing God to men so that men can become gods, Mormonism distorts the nature of God and perverts the gospel of Christ.

ADDITIONAL THOUGHTS:

Other verses the Mormon Church cites in support of their doctrine of men becoming gods are **Acts 17:29** where the apostle Paul declares "we are the offspring of God" and **Romans 8:16-17** where he states, "**we are the children of God**: And if children, then heirs; heirs of God, and **joint-heirs with Christ**." Yet these passages are speaking of adoption into God's spiritual family and "heirs" of His kingdom through faith in Christ (**John 1:12**), not eternal progression. **Isaiah 14:12-14** says, "How art thou fallen from heaven, **O Lucifer**...For thou hast said in thine heart... I will **exalt** my throne above the stars of God...I will be **like** the most High." Lucifer fell for trying to be "like" God, so why would anyone want to follow his example?

Is God a Trinity?

A distinct difference between Mormonism and Christianity is how the character and nature of God are defined. Mormons deny the Christian doctrine of the Trinity of God being three distinct persons in One Being, and they teach, instead, that the Godhead is comprised of three separate gods.

When Lee and I left Mormonism, we struggled finding a Christian church because the idea of the Trinity didn't make sense to us. We thought God the Father had a physical human body as an exalted man, as Mormonism teaches; and since Jesus also possesses a human body, we could not understand how they could both be one God.

Then we learned that the Bible teaches that **God is not a man**[1] and that **He is a Spirit**,[2] and that the only person of the Godhead who has a physical body is Jesus Christ.[3]

Since God is Spirit, the Bible teaches that no person has ever seen God,[4] and this is why Jesus told Philip, "...he that hath seen me hath seen the Father."[5] Because Jesus is the "image

---

[1] Hosea 11:9
[2] John 4:24
[3] Philippians 2:6-8
[4] See John 1:18; John 5:37; John 6:47
[5] John 14:9

of the invisible God" (Colossians 1:15), the Bible explains that all the fullness of Deity dwells in Him bodily (Colossians 2:9).

In this way, we see the Christian doctrine of the Trinity clearly taught in the Bible where not only is the **Father** called God (1 Peter 1:2), but **Jesus** is God (John 1:1, 20:28, Colossians 2:9) and so is the **Holy Spirit** (Acts 5:3-4). Yet, God says, "**I am God, and there is no other**; I am God, and **there is no one like Me**." (Isaiah 46:9). "I *am* He, **I *am* the first, I also *am* the last**." (Isaiah 48:12). "I am **Alpha** and **Omega**, the **beginning** and the **ending**, saith the Lord...**the Almighty**." (Revelation 1:8)

By teaching multiple gods, Mormonism misrepresents the character of the true God, described in the Bible, and cannot be considered Christian.

ADDITIONAL THOUGHTS:

TRINITY IN THE SCRIPTURES

The Trinity is not Modalism—the view that the Father, Son, and Holy Spirit are all one person; nor is it Tritheism—the view that the Father, Son and Holy Spirit are three separate Gods. It is the teaching that the three persons are distinct in their personhood, yet existing in one Being, who is God. We can see the concept of Trinity (three persons in one God) revealed in the following verse:

Matthew 28:19: "Go therefore and make disciples of all the nations, baptizing them in **the name** of **the Father** and **the Son** and **the Holy Spirit**...."

Notice that the word "name" is singular (not plural i.e., "names"). Also, the definite article "the" is placed in front of "the Father, the Son, and the Holy Spirit," thus, implying plurality within unity.

Although the Trinity cannot be totally comprehended, it can be apprehended and seen illustrated in the world of nature. Take, for example, an illustration involving three candles. Even after lighting each candle, they are still distinct. However, when one combines each of the three flames together, they become one flame. In the same way, each member of the Trinity is distinct in His personhood, yet they are one Being we call "God."

We can see the Trinity in the Mormon KJV Bible where they state in their *LDS Bible Dictionary* on page 681, "When one **speaks of God, it is generally the Father** who is referred to; **that is, Elohim**... The personage known as **Jehovah...is usually identified in the Old Testament as LORD (in capital letters), is the Son**, known as **Jesus Christ**, who is also **a God**."

Using this rule of interpretation where "God" or "*Elohim*" in the Hebrew text would be translated "Father" and "LORD" or "*Jehovah*" in the Hebrew text would be translated "Jesus," let's examine the following verses:

Psalm 2:7: "I will declare the decree: the **LORD [Jehovah] hath said** unto me, **Thou** *art* **my Son**; this day have I begotten thee."

Here we see that God the Father and His Son Jehovah Jesus are the SAME God.

Isaiah 43:10; 44:8: "...**saith the LORD** [Jehovah]...**understand** that I am he: **before me there was no God [Elohim] formed**, neither shall there be after me... Is there a God [Elohim] beside me? Yea, **there is no God** [Elohim]; **I know not** *any*."

Since no "God" Elohim (Father) was formed BEFORE the "LORD" Jehovah (Jesus), how can they be two separate "Gods" ?

Another question that a person can ask a Mormon who believes in three separate Gods is:

Who do you worship? Do you worship the Father or the Son? Who did the Disciples worship in the Bible? Who did the Nephites worship in the Book of Mormon? Since they worshipped Christ, why don't you worship Him? If you do worship Christ along with the Father, are you worshipping TWO Gods instead of One?

Matthew 28:17: "···And when they saw him, they worshipped him."

NOTE: Unlike angels (Revelation 22:8-9) and men (Acts 10:25-26) who refused worship, Jesus never rejected it (Revelation 5:11-14; Hebrews 1:6).

1 Nephi 11:24: "···I beheld the Son of God and I saw many fall down at his feet and worship him." - *Book of Mormon*

3 Nephi 11:17: "···And they did fall down at the feet of Jesus, and did worship him." *–Book of Mormon*

Amulek, the true prophet of God in the Book of Mormon, was asked, **"Is there more than one [true and living] God?"** (Alma 11:26-28) What do you think His answer was to this?

Alma 11:28-29: "Now Zeezrom said: **Is there more than one God?** And he answered, **No**."

See also the following Book of Mormon Scriptures:

Alma 11:44: "...shall be brought and be arraigned before the bar of Christ the Son, and God the Father, and the Holy Spirit, which is **one Eternal God**."

2 Nephi 11:7: "For **if there be no Christ there be no God**; and if there be no God we are not, for there could have been no creation. But **there is a God, and he is Christ**, and he cometh in the fulness of his own time.

2 Nephi 31:21: "···this is the doctrine of Christ, and the only and true doctrine of the Father, and of the Son, and of the Holy Ghost, which is **one God**, without end. Amen."

3 Nephi 11:27, 36: "the Father, and the Son, and the Holy Ghost are one; and I am in the Father, and the Father in me, and the Father and I are one. for **the Father, and I, and the Holy Ghost are one**."

Mosiah 15:1-4: "**God himself shall come down** among the children of men, and shall redeem his people. ···being the Father and the Son ···The Father, because he was conceived by the power of God; and the Son, because of the flesh; thus becoming the Father and Son— And **they are one God**, yea, the very Eternal Father of heaven and of earth."

At Matthew 1:18-20 we read that Mary was "found with child of the Holy Ghost for that which is conceived in her is of the Holy Ghost."

If the Holy Ghost is a separate God from the Father (as Mormonism teaches), why is Jesus called the "Son of God" rather than being called the "Son of the Holy Ghost"? **Doesn't this prove that the Father and the Holy Ghost are the same God?**

Do Mormons Believe Jesus and Lucifer are Brothers?

Mormons teach that Jesus is the brother of Lucifer. They believe that the spirits of Jesus and Lucifer were first born to Heavenly Father in heaven that Mormons call the pre-existence. According to Mormon Scripture, Jesus was the first one born and Lucifer was the second one and then all the other spirits of humans and angels were born.

Not only do Mormons teach that Jesus and Satan are brothers, they teach that there was a contest between Jesus and Lucifer over who would become Savior of the world. According to Mormonism, God chose Jesus' plan over Lucifer's plan and as a result Lucifer became angry and fell, and took a third of the spirit children with him, becoming Satan and the demons.

As a Mormon, I would get upset whenever I heard someone doubting whether Mormons are Christians. I took offense that anyone would question my belief in Jesus Christ. What I didn't realize was that the Jesus that the Mormon Church teaches is completely different from the Jesus of the Bible.

The difference between Jesus and Lucifer in the Bible is the difference between Creator and Creation. Jesus is the creator of "all things" (Colossians 1:15-18) and as such, He is Lucifer's

Creator. Being fully God, the Creator as the Bible teaches in **John 1:1-3**, and therefore Jesus created Lucifer and never competed with him for the position of Savior of the World.

The Apostle Paul warned in the Bible against following those who "preacheth another Jesus, whom we have not preached." (2 Corinthians 11:4) By misrepresenting the nature of Christ, Mormonism distorts the gospel and cannot be considered Christian.

ADDITIONAL THOUGHTS:

Mormonism makes no distinction between human spirits and angelic beings. For example, in Mormonism, the Angel Moroni is supposedly a resurrected human from the Book of Mormon. Yet, the Bible teaches that humans cannot become angels because we are a completely separate creation. In **Hebrews 2:9, 16-17**, we read that by becoming a human, Jesus "was **made like unto *his* brethren ...a little lower than the angels**." Now, if angels are disembodied human spirits, how could Jesus be "made...lower than the angels" by becoming a human? These biblical statements wouldn't make sense if angles are disembodied human spirits. Again, a clear distinction is made between angels and humans when we read that Jesus did not take upon Himself the "the nature of angels," but took upon Himself the "the seed of Abraham," (that is, human nature) in order to pay for our sins (Hebrews 2:16).

Did Humans Preexist in Heaven?

Did we preexist as spirits in heaven before we were born on earth as Mormonism teaches?

When Kathy and I left Mormonism, we learned that the Mormon doctrine of premortal life is not found in the Bible and that it is not even taught in the Book of Mormon. The only real support for the Mormon belief in a preexistence is found in the Mormon Scripture, the Book of Abraham, which Joseph Smith created from an Egyptian burial manuscript.

While no Bible-believing Christian today believes in our preexistence, that doesn't stop the Mormon Church from trying to find verses in the Bible to support this false belief by citing several Scriptures, which show, that Jesus existed in heaven before He came to earth. (See *New Era,* Feb. 1972 Question & Answers)

Of course, Jesus preexisted in Heaven because He is fully God (Philippians 2:5-9) and has always existed, "having **neither beginning of days**, nor end of life... " as it says in **Hebrews 7:3**. But Jesus Himself taught that there is a difference between Himself and all of us when He said to the people around Him: "Ye are **from beneath**; **I am from above**: ye are **of this world**; **I am not of this world**." (John 8:23). By telling them that they are not from Heaven like He is, He showed that no human person (but Himself) can claim preexistence in Heaven.

Another Bible verse that disproves premortal life is **1 Corinthians 15:46-47** which says, "Howbeit that was **not first** which is spiritual, but that which is natural; and **afterward** that which is spiritual. The **first man** is **of the earth**, earthy: the **second man** is the **Lord from heaven**."

Other Bible verses that the Mormon Church cites to try to support this false belief can be easily refuted by examining them in context. By misrepresenting the beliefs of the Bible, Mormonism cannot be considered Christian.

ADDITIONAL THOUGHTS:

The Mormon Church cites **Jeremiah 1:5** where God tells Jeremiah that He "knew" him before he was formed in the womb. Yet, this doesn't prove preexistence because God is all-knowing, so He **"calleth those things which be not as though they were" (Romans 4:17)**. Likewise, Jesus also disproved premortal life when He told the Jews at **John 5:37**, "the Father himself, which hath sent me, hath borne witness of me. **Ye have neither heard his voice at any time, nor seen his shape.**" And at **John 1:18**, Jesus tells us that, **"No man hath seen God at any time."** See also **John 6:46**. If we all preexisted in Heaven as spirit-children of God before we were born on earth, we would have seen God or at least heard His voice. This is why the Bible teaches at **Zechariah 12:1** that our spirits were created within our bodies.

Will Families Be Together Forever in Heaven?

Mormons believe that after death, all good people will end up in one of three kingdoms of glory: the celestial kingdom, for the most faithful Mormons, the terrestrial, for good people who were not as worthy, and the telestial kingdom for people who refused the gospel.

When Lee and I were LDS, we strived hard to attain to the celestial glory because we were taught that if we were worthy enough, we would live together with our family forever in this kingdom. But when Lee began to have questions and doubts about Mormonism, my hopes for our family being together in eternity began to fall apart.

Lee was sitting right next to me when our Bishop said to me in his office, "Don't worry if Lee leaves Mormonism, we can find a worthy priesthood holder for you."

I was shocked! I didn't want him to find a new husband for me. I wanted him to answer Lee's questions so that we could stay together as a family in heaven. Eventually Lee's questions became my questions and we learned that the reason our Bishop couldn't answer our questions was because there are no good answers for the problems in Mormonism.

Since we've left the LDS Church, we've learned

that heaven is not divided in to 3 Kingdoms that will separate unworthy family members from each other. The Bible teaches that all of us have sinned and fall short of the glory of God (Romans 3:23), and it is by our faith in Jesus Christ that makes us all able to live together forever in one Kingdom of Heaven (Romans 6:23; Matthew 25:46).

When the Bible speaks of **three Heavens**, it is only referring to, **the sky** - one heaven (Genesis 1:20, Revelation 19:17), **space** - the second heaven (Psalm 19:1), and **God's Kingdom, the third heaven** (2 Corinthians 12:2). By distorting the gospel, Mormonism cannot be consider Christian.

ADDITIONAL THOUGHTS:

The Mormon idea that marriage can extend into eternity was disputed by the teachings of Christ. In Matthew 22:29-30, when Jesus was told about a woman who had been married to seven husbands on the earth, he was asked:

> "**Therefore in the resurrection whose wife shall she be of the seven? for they all had her**. Jesus answered and said unto them, Ye do err, not knowing the scriptures, nor the power of God. **For in the resurrection they neither marry, nor are given in marriage**, but are as the angels of God in heaven."

CHAPTER FOUR:

MORMONISM AND THE RESTORATION

"If we cannot convince you by reason nor by the word of God, that your religion is wrong, we will not persecute you... we ask from you the same generosity...convince us of our errors of doctrine, if we have any, by reason, by logical arguments, or by the word of God, and we will be ever grateful for the information."

—Orson Pratt (Apostle)
(The Seer, Vol. 1, 1853, 1990 edition, p. 15)

No Need for a Prophet Today

Have you ever wondered why the Church of Jesus Christ of Latter-day Saints, that is, the Mormon Church, has a living prophet leading their church while Bible-believing Christian churches do not?

Bible at Amos 3:7 says, "Surely the Lord GOD will do nothing, but he revealeth his secret unto his servants the prophets." Leaders of the Mormon Church teach that "the Lord keeps a **channel of communication** open to His children through" their living prophet and that by "sustaining" their church leaders, "the Lord will never" allow their church members "to be led astray."[1]

Is it true that without the revelations of a modern-day prophet, God's people would be led astray?

No! The Bible says in Hebrews chapter one: "God... spake **in time past** unto the fathers by the prophets, **hath in these last days spoken unto us by his Son**." Likewise, **Luke 16:16** states, "The law and **the prophets were until John**: since that time the kingdom of God is preached, and every man presseth into it."

What these Scriptures are saying is that up until the time of Christ, God used prophets to speak

---

[1] See October 1994, General Conference talk entitled, *Heed the Prophet's Voice,* at lds.org.

to His people, but now through Christ, every Christian, has direct access to personal revelation from God through His Holy Spirit.

In John 14:26: Jesus promised, "But the Comforter, **which is the Holy Ghost**, whom the Father will send in my name, **he shall teach you all things**, and bring all things to your remembrance, whatsoever I have said unto you."

By following the revelations of modern-day prophets instead of the divine revelations of Christ's Holy Spirit and the Bible, Mormonism distorts the gospel and cannot be considered Christian.

ADDITIONAL THOUGHTS:

Ephesians 2:20 declares that the Christian church is built upon the "foundation" of the "apostles" and "prophets." These people were unique in their ability to write "Scripture" because they had physically seen Jesus Christ (1 Corinthians 9:1-2). Yet now, the "foundation" of the Christian church has been laid with their writings recorded in the Bible. Thus, there is no need for additional prophets and apostles to write Scripture, for once a house "foundation" is laid, there is no need to rebuild it. Yet, in a limited sense, non-foundational "prophets" and "apostles" serve today as Christian missionaries and pastors proclaiming God's Word.[2]

---

[2] See 1 Corinthians 12:28; Acts 13:1.

No Need for a Restored Gospel

What is the gospel or Good News? **1 Corinthians 15:1-4** says that the gospel consists of belief in Jesus Christ's death for our sins, His burial and His Resurrection. But did you know that most Mormons today think that this simple gospel taught in the Bible is incomplete?

Yes, the Mormon Church claims that when the first-century Christian Apostles died, many "plain and most precious" truths of the gospel were lost and that Joseph Smith was called by God to "restore" what was missing in the Christian gospel.

So what makes the Mormon "**restored**" gospel different from the biblical gospel?

Mormon Priesthood Authority: When I (Lee) was a Bishop in the Mormon Church, I taught that Christians who are not ordained to the Mormon Aaronic and Melchizedek priesthoods do not have the authority to operate with the power of God.

And when I (Kathy) was growing up in the Mormon Church, I believed that I had to perform special temple ordinances, such as being married for time and eternity, before I could go to the Highest Kingdom of Heaven.

But are these additions to the gospel a true "restoration" of the first-century gospel?

No! Not a single wedding was ever performed in the biblical temple and neither Jesus nor His Apostles held the Aaronic Priesthood because they were not Levites. So how can the Mormon gospel be a true restoration? Obviously, Mormonism is a counterfeit gospel and falls under the condemnation of Galatians 1:9: "If any *man* preach **any other gospel** unto you... let him be accursed."

ADDITIONAL THOUGHTS:

Not only are Mormonism's "restored" teachings not found in the Bible, but they are missing in the Book of Mormon as well. Therefore, Mormonism falls under the condemnation of Jesus in its own Book of Mormon who says at **3 Nephi 11:39-40**, "Verily, verily, I say unto you, that this is my doctrine ...and **whoso shall declare more or less than this**, and establish it for my doctrine, the same cometh of evil..." The Bible is clear that the "gospel" that was delivered to the Christian saints would never be lost from the earth (Matthew 16:18). **Jude 3** exhorts believers to, "contend for the faith: which was **once delivered** unto the saints." According to *Strong's Concordance,* the Greek word (ἅπαξ - *hápax*) translated "once" means "one (or a single) time." So in other words, the gospel was delivered "once" and for all time. Likewise, Hebrews 12:28 says, "we receiving a **kingdom which cannot be moved**, ...may serve God acceptably..." The gospel was delivered once for all and the kingdom was not moved from the earth, so there is no need for a restoration.

No Need for a Restoration of Gospel Authority

By what authority do you or your Christian pastor perform gospel ordinances, such as baptizing new believers or laying hands on someone to receive the Holy Spirit? Mormons often challenge Christians with this question because they believe that gospel "authority" was lost when the Apostles died and that it had to be "restored" through their Prophet Joseph Smith. But what does the Bible say?

In Matthew chapter 28, Jesus told His followers, "**All authority** in heaven and on earth has been given to me. **Therefore go** and make disciples of **all nations**, **baptizing** them ... And surely **I am with you always, to the very end of the age**." (Matthew 28:17-19, *New International Version*)

Because Jesus holds "**All authority**" and has promised to be "**with**" Christians "**always...to the very end**," how could gospel priesthood authority be lost from the earth for 18 centuries until Joseph Smith "restored" it?

Not only was authority **not** lost with the death of the apostles, it had been transferred to thousands of new believers in Acts, who received the Holy Spirit at Pentecost the moment that they first believed. This priesthood authority of all believers, or "power" as it is also called, has allowed Christians of all centuries to carry the message of Christ "to the uttermost parts of the earth." (Acts 1:8)

This is why the "authority" to carry out gospel ordinances that Jesus transferred directly to the apostles, was no longer limited to them, and as a result, that authority was never lost when they died.

Indeed, we can be confident that Jesus fulfilled His promise to us when he said that He would build His church and the "gates of hell shall not prevail against it." (Matthew 16:18)

ADDITIONAL THOUGHTS:

Acts 3:19–21 speaks of the "restitution of all things" and is often presented as biblical proof for the Mormon restoration. Yet, this passage discusses a restitution that will occur just before Jesus' second coming and says that heaven must receive him "until the times of restitution of all things." The Apostle Paul explained that at the "glorious appearing" of Jesus Christ, Jesus will "redeem" and purify His people, the sons and daughters of God (Titus 2:13-14). Then, when these children of God are manifested, all of creation "shall be delivered from the bondage of corruption" due to the curse (Romans 8:19-22). Thus, the context of Acts 3:19-21 has nothing to do with a "restitution" of the "gospel", but rather, it is talking about the prophesied "restitution of all things" in creation when it will be delivered from the curse "when... he shall send Jesus Christ" (Acts 3:20) back to earth to reign (Revelation 19-22).

No Need for a Restored Priesthood

Does Mormonism restore the Aaronic and Melchizedek Priesthoods mentioned in the Bible?

Joseph Smith claimed that he was ordained to the Aaronic and Melchizedek Priesthoods through a special visitation of the biblical patriarchs who gave him these Priesthoods to be passed down to the male members of the Church through ordination.

When I was ordained as a Bishop of the Mormon Church, I took pride in the fact that **my Priesthood Line of Authority went back to the former Mormon Prophet Thomas S. Monson** with only one man between me and him! What I did not realize was that it was all a lie. No man in the Bible ever held both Priesthoods, and I wasn't even qualified, under biblical standards, to hold these Priesthoods. Even Jesus Himself was not qualified to hold the Aaronic Priesthood. So how could I claim to hold something that Jesus could not hold?

The Bible explains at Hebrews chapter 7: "For **the priesthood being changed**, there is made of necessity a change also of the law.... For *it is* evident that **our Lord sprang out of Juda**; of which tribe Moses spake **nothing** concerning priesthood."[1]

Because Jesus was not of the tribe of Levi, the only way He could function as our High Priest

---

[1] See Hebrews 7:12-14.

115

was for Him to be ordained to a completely different Priesthood, the Priesthood of Melchizedek (Hebrews 7:21).

And because Christ lives forever, the Bible says, "he hath an unchangeable priesthood." This priesthood is called "unchangeable" because it doesn't "change" hands from one person to another. In other words, it is a **non-transferable**, priesthood.

So how could I as a Mormon believe that I held the Melchizedek Priesthood when it was not transferable from Jesus to me? Because Christ is our only High Priest, we do not need Mormon Aaronic and Melchizedek "High Priests" to stand between us and God.

ADDITIONAL THOUGHTS:

As we have seen, Jesus Christ could not hold the Aaronic Priesthood because He was not a descendent of Aaron, so neither could Joseph Smith because he "was of the lineage of Joseph through the loins of Ephraim."[2] In the Bible, only one high priest served at a time so only one priesthood was in power at one time. Thus, when Jesus received all authority after His resurrection, the Aaronic priesthood authority was replaced by the greater Melchizedek Priesthood (Hebrews 7:11-17). Because Jesus lives forever (Hebrews 7:24), the Aaronic Priesthood authority has forever been abolished.

---

[2] See *Doctrines of Salvation*, vol. 3, p. 247

No Need for Restored Temples

Have you ever wondered why the Mormon Church, builds temples throughout the world? What exactly do the Mormons do in their temples?

Mormons believe that they must perform secret temple rituals in order to gain eternal life. These rituals include temple workers washing and anointing specific body parts of the person going through the temple, the giving of secret names, handshakes, and temple garments which Mormons are expected to wear under their clothing for the rest of their lives.

Other temple activities that Lee and I participated in when we were Mormons, included getting baptized for our dead relatives and marriage for time and eternity.

In spite of the fact that the Mormon Church claims that their temples are a "restoration" of the biblical temple, there is absolutely **no resemblance** between the biblical temple that existed in Jesus' day and Mormon temples today. Not only are the furnishings and structures of the Mormon temples completely incompatible with the biblical temple, but none of the Mormon temple rituals were ever performed in the biblical temple.

And what about the Mormon belief in temple Marriage for eternity? Was Jesus married? What about the Apostle Paul? How could anyone get married in the biblical temple when women were not allowed past the "court of women" in the Jewish temple? Jesus even condemned this belief in eternal marriage when He said, "in the resurrection they neither marry, nor **are given in marriage**, but are as the angels of God in heaven" (Matt. 22:28-30).

By adding temple works to faith in Christ, Mormonism distorts the gospel of Christ and cannot be considered Christian.

ADDITIONAL THOUGHTS:

The Jews were given specific details on how to build the Jewish temple in Jerusalem. There was to be no other location for the temple, and the details were to be carried out with precision because the Jewish priest were to serve, "at a sanctuary that is **a copy and shadow of what is in heaven**. This is why Moses was warned when he was about to build the tabernacle: 'See to it that you **make everything according to the pattern shown you on the mountain.**' " (Hebrews 8:5, NIV) So when the Mormon Church distorts this picture of the heavenly temple by changing its design on earth, they are in violation of God's pattern. Today, Christians no longer need a temple for worship because our "bodies are the temple of the Holy Spirit" (1 Corinthians 3:16-17), and we no longer need to worship God at a specific temple location but in spirit and in truth (John 4:20-24).

No Need for Baptism for the Dead

Have you ever been baptized for your dead relatives?

A Christian can't answer this question because baptism for the dead is not something that is practiced within the churches of Christianity, but in over 150 Mormon temples worldwide, faithful Mormons are being baptized vicariously for their dead relatives in the hopes of increasing their chances of salvation in the next life.

But is baptism for the dead a biblical practice? What about 1 Corinthians 15:29 where the Apostle Paul says, "Else what shall **they** do which are baptized for the dead...?"

If the Bible teaches this doctrine, why did the Apostle Paul exclude himself and the people he was writing to when he said, "what shall **they** do" instead of "what shall **we** do"? History shows that no Jew or Christian was ever baptized for the dead in the biblical temple. In fact, the writings of an early Church father, Clement of Alexandria, even attributed baptism for the dead to a heretical practice of a Gnostic sect.[1]

But what about redeeming our dead relatives? Doesn't the Bible teach that people who did not accept the gospel prior to death will have a second chance to get saved after they die?

---

[1] See: Clement of Alexandria, Saint, ca. AD 153 to 217; Referenced at http://mit.irr.org/ancient-gnostic-heretics-and-baptism-dead.

No! The Bible Says at Hebrews 9:27, "it is appointed unto men **once to die**, but after this the judgment." Even the *Book of Mormon* teaches at Alma 35, "For behold, **this life** is the time for men to prepare to meet God ... . For behold, if ye have procrastinated the day of your repentance even until death, behold, ye have become subjected to the spirit of the devil, and he doth seal you his."[2] Also, Psalm 49:7 warns, "None of them can by any means **redeem his brother**, nor give to God a ransom for him." By teaching baptism for the dead, Mormonism distorts the gospel of Christ and cannot be considered Christian.

ADDITIONAL THOUGHTS:

Contrary to the claims of Mormonism, physical baptism is not a pre-requisite for salvation. At Luke 23:43, we read that Jesus assured the thief on the cross (who had not been baptized), that he would be "with" Him in paradise (heaven) that day, simply because he believed. The Apostle Paul made a distinction between the "gospel" and "baptism" when he proclaimed to the Corinthian believers, "I thank God that I baptized none of you. ...For Christ sent me **not to baptize**, but to preach the gospel." (1 Corinthians 1:14, 17) Not only does Paul reject the notion that "baptism" was part of the "gospel," but he repeatedly affirmed salvation by "faith" apart from works (Romans 4:5, 11:6).

---

[2] Alma 35:32, 35.

No Need for a Restored Bible

Did you know that Mormons believe that the Bible that Christians read today is not accurate?

The Mormon Church's 8th Article of Faith states: "We believe the Bible to be the word of God **as far as it is translated correctly**."

So convinced was Joseph Smith that the Bible had been incorrectly "translated," that he created his own translation of the Bible called the "Inspired Version" or "Joseph Smith Translation" where he added and revised whole sections of the Bible without any support from the ancient manuscripts.

One change Joseph Smith made to his version of the Bible is at Genesis chapter 17 where God makes a covenant with Abraham, requiring circumcision at "eight days" old. Although this covenant was performed for centuries by all biblical prophets up through the time of Christ, Joseph Smith changed it from "eight days" to "eight years" and this change forms the basis of the Mormon practice of baptism at "eight years," even though the context of the passage speaks of circumcision, and not baptism.

Does this make any sense to you? **Would God really wait over 3,000 years of His Prophets and His Son performing the first covenant wrong until Joseph Smith comes along and corrects it** in **his** Bible? This is not the only serious change Joseph Smith made to his version of the Bible. He also added a whole series of verses to the last chapter of Genesis prophesying about himself in an attempt to solidify his calling as a prophet.

At Deuteronomy 4:2, God warns against those who would add or take away from His Word. If a church removes, restricts or rewrites the Word of God, then that church can and will teach, preach and practice anything in the name of God.

ADDITIONAL THOUGHTS:

Other changes Joseph Smith made to his version of the Bible include **Exodus 33:20** where Moses could not see God's face and live. Joseph changed this to say that Moses could not see God's face if he remained in his sinful state. Joseph Smith also changed **Romans 4:5** to say that God does "not" justify the ungodly, and he changed **John 1:1** to read that the Son was "of" God, rather than being God Himself. Although Smith's Book of Mormon states at 1 Nephi 13:32 that "plain and most precious parts of the gospel" were removed from the Bible by the so-called "abominable church," God promised us in the Bible that His Word would endure forever. "The grass withereth, the flower fadeth: but the word of our God shall stand for ever" (Isaiah 40:8). "For verily I say unto you, Till heaven and earth pass, one jot or one tittle shall in no wise pass from the law, till all be fulfilled" (Matthew 5:18).

CHAPTER FIVE:

MORMONISM AND THE FIVE SOLAS OF CHRISTIANITY

The five solas (from the Latin word "sola," meaning "alone") are the foundational set of biblical teachings that grew out of the Protestant Reformation.

Christian pastors and theologians have historically claimed that these teachings are central to the gospel as proclaimed in the Bible in contrast to the teachings of the Roman Catholic Church.

In this section, we will contrast these historically Christian beliefs against the teachings of the Mormon Church.

By Faith Alone

"Sola Fide" (Sola Fe-day), **"By Faith Alone"** is one of the "five solas," or five essential doctrines, of the historic Christian faith that is completely distorted within Mormonism. To a Christian, **"By Faith Alone"** means that you are saved by your belief in the sacrificial death of Jesus Christ alone, excluding any works of your own for your salvation.

True Christians trust in the Bible when it says in *Ephesians 2:8-9*, "For it is by **grace** you have been saved, through **faith** – and this is **not from yourselves**, it is the **gift of God** – not by **works, so that no one can boast."

Yet, Mormonism teaches a grace plus works doctrine. In the Book of Mormon at **2 Nephi 25:23**, it says, "for we know that it is by grace that we are saved, **after** all we can do." **After all we can do?** This is definitely **not** a Christian belief! Mormon leaders have even gone so far as to claim that this doctrine of "faith alone" was "originated by Satan" himself!

Now ask yourself, "How can the Mormon Church be considered Christian when they teach that man is **not saved** by the doctrine of faith alone?" This doctrine forms the **very** foundation of the biblical gospel. To deny salvation by faith alone is to reject the **full sufficiency** of Christ's atonement. By teaching that Faith Alone is not enough, Mormons claim you must work your way to the highest level of heaven by being temple-worthy and obeying certain laws and ordinances set up by the Mormon Church. These include tithing a full 10% of your income and being baptized by a man holding the Mormon Melchizedek Priesthood.

Yet, the Bible says in **Romans 10:9**: If you declare **with your mouth, "Jesus is Lord,"** and believe in your heart that **God raised him** from the dead, you will be saved." We want you to know that belief in **Jesus Christ Alone is sufficient for your salvation.** You are saved by faith... **not** by your works, so that no one can boast!

ADDITIONAL THOUGHTS:

At what point can a Mormon be confident that he has done enough works to receive salvation? **Moroni 10:32** in the Book of Mormon claims that you must, "...**deny yourselves of all ungodliness**; and **if** ye shall deny yourselves of all ungodliness...**then** is his grace sufficient for you, that by his grace ye may be perfect in Christ." **Alma 11:37** says that Jesus, "...**cannot save them in their sins** ...no unclean thing can inherit the kingdom of heaven. ...Therefore, **ye cannot be saved in your sins.**" **Alma 5:27** states, "Have ye walked, keeping yourselves **blameless before God**? Could ye say, if ye were called to die at this time, within yourselves, that ye have been **sufficiently humble**? ...Behold, are ye **stripped of pride**? I say unto you, if ye are not ye are **not prepared** to meet God."

By Grace Alone

"Sola Gratia" which is Latin for **"By Grace Alone**," is one of the essential doctrines of the Christian faith that cannot be found within the Mormon Church. The Bible says at *Ephesians 2:8-9*, "For it is by **grace** you have been saved, through faith – and this is **not from yourselves**, it is the **gift of God** – **not** by **works,** so that no one can boast."

The grace that we receive for salvation is a **"gift of God** – **not** by **works**." The Bible goes on to explain at **Romans 11:6** "And if **by grace, then is it no more of works**: **otherwise grace is no more grace**. But if *it be* of works, then is it **no more grace**: otherwise work is no more work."

In other words, there is a clear distinction between salvation by works and salvation by grace. Either you are trusting your works, or you are trusting in Grace Alone to save you. You cannot have it both ways. When the Mormon Church adds works to grace for salvation, they change the very definition of grace. In fact, the LDS Bible Dictionary, actually says under the heading "Grace" on page 697, "This **grace is an enabling power** that allows men and women to lay hold on eternal life and exaltation **after** **they have expended their own best efforts**."

"After they have expended their own best efforts"? How does that definition fit with the biblical definition of grace, "if **by grace, then** *is* *it* **no more of works**"? Not only does Mormonism distort the meaning of grace, but Joseph Smith, changed it in his own Bible translation of Romans 4:5 where we read that God "justifieth the ungodly." Instead, Joseph Smith wrote, God "justifieth **not** the ungodly." But if God does not justify the ungodly, how can anyone be saved? By changing the very definition of Grace, Mormonism distorts the gospel of Christ and cannot be considered Christian.

ADDITIONAL THOUGHTS:

At what point can any Mormon be confident he has repented enough to be guaranteed forgiveness? **Doctrine and Covenants 1:31-32** states, "For I the Lord **cannot look upon sin with the least degree of allowance**; Nevertheless, he that **repents** and does the commandments of the Lord shall be forgiven." **Doctrine and Covenants 58:46** and **82:7** claim, "By this ye may know if a man **repenteth** of his sins—behold, he will confess them and **forsake them**. ...go your ways and **sin no more**; but unto that soul who sinneth shall **the former sins return**, saith the Lord your God." Have you ever repeated a sin after asking for forgiveness? The Mormon Church warns, "Those who receive forgiveness and then **repeat the sin are held accountable for their former sins**." (*Gospel Principles,* 1995, p. 253) Can you see why biblical forgiveness must be unconditional (Ps. 103:12)?

In Christ Alone

"*Solus Christus*" which is Latin for "In Christ Alone" is another essential doctrine of the Christian faith that is completely rejected by the Mormon Church. "**In Christ Alone**" means that Christians trust in **Jesus Christ Alone** for salvation and do not put faith in any other person to stand between them and God.

The Bible teaches at *1 Timothy 2:5*, "For there is **one God**, and **one mediator** between God and men, the man **Christ Jesus**." But the Mormon Church rejects this truth when they add their prophet Joseph Smith to the redemption plan of Christ.

Instead of trusting in Jesus Christ alone, the Mormon Church states in their June 1994, *Ensign* article entitled, "Joseph Smith among the Prophets" that "...the life of Joseph Smith was in some degree patterned after that of his Master, Jesus Christ. Like his Master, **Joseph Smith also shed his blood** in order that the final testament, the reestablishment of the new covenant, **might be in full effect**."[1]

Now wait a minute! Does the Mormon Church **really** teach that the **blood of Joseph Smith** was necessary for the full "reestablishment of the new covenant"?

Absolutely! And in this article they also quote their prophet Brigham Young who taught, "**No**

---

[1] *Ensign,* June 1994, p. 22

man or woman in this dispensation will ever **enter** into the celestial kingdom of God **without the consent of Joseph Smith**... every man and woman must have the **certificate of Joseph Smith, junior, as a passport** to their entrance into the mansion where God and Christ are."

If that's not blasphemy, I don't know what is!

By adding Joseph Smith to the redemption plan of Christ, Mormonism distorts the gospel of Christ and cannot be considered Christian.

ADDITIONAL THOUGHTS:

Another way Mormonism rejects the doctrine of "Christ Alone" is by teaching the blood of Jesus is insufficient to cover all sin, particularly murder. **Doctrine and Covenants 42:18** states, "Thou shalt not kill; and **he that kills shall not have forgiveness in this world, nor in the world to come**." Joseph Fielding Smith, acknowledged, "Joseph Smith taught that there were certain sins so grievous that man may commit, that they will **place the transgressors beyond the power of the atonement of Christ**."[2] This doctrine known as "blood atonement,"[3] clearly disagrees with the Bible's teachings on the sufficiency of Christ's atonement and testimony of the apostle Paul who was forgiven for murder (1 Cor. 15:9-10).

[2] Joseph Fielding Smith, *Doctrines of Salvation,* vol 1, p. 135.
[3] See Footnote 6 of the LDS Gospel Topics Essay, "Peace and Violence Among 19th Century Latter-day Saints" published at lds.org

By Scripture Alone

"*Sola Scriptura*" which is Latin for "**Scripture Alone**" is a fundamental doctrine of the historic Christian faith that is completely rejected by the Mormon Church. "Scripture Alone" means that Christians regard the teachings of the Bible as the final authority for determining the doctrines and practices of the Christian faith.

The Bible says at *2 Timothy 3:16* that "**All scripture** is given by inspiration of God, and is profitable for **doctrine**... for **instruction** in righteousness." But the Book of Mormon rejects this truth when it mocks Christians who trust in the Bible Alone, saying at **2 Nephi 29:6**, "Thou **fool**, that shall say: **A Bible, we have got a Bible, and we need no more Bible.**"

Not only does Mormonism reject "Scripture Alone," but it claims that "there are **many plain and precious things taken away from the book**, which is the **book of the Lamb of God**" (1 Nephi 13:28), and their 8th Article of Faith says, "We believe the Bible to be the word of God **as far as it is translated correctly**... ."

By questioning the accuracy and transmission of the biblical text, Mormonism rejects the promise of Christ who said at Matthew 24:35, "Heaven and earth shall pass away, but **my words shall not pass away.**"

Not only is the preservation of the biblical text defended by the very promise of Christ, but it has been verified by the archaeological discoveries of ancient manuscripts that, when compared with the biblical text, all agree with **99% accuracy.**

By teaching that Jesus failed to preserve His Word in the Bible, Mormonism distorts the doctrines of Christ and cannot be considered Christian.

ADDITIONAL THOUGHTS:

Evidence of Biblical Preservation:

- **24,000+** partial and complete New Testament manuscripts including 5,000+ original Greek manuscripts, some dated within 100 years of the original writings, all agree with 99% accuracy.

- From **36,000+ quotations** of the New Testament **from early Church Fathers** before the 4th century, one can **reconstruct the entire New Testament**, except 11 insignificant verses.

- Discovery of the **Hebrew Old Testament manuscripts** found in the Dead Sea Scrolls (125 B.C.) compared with copies written **1,000 years later** (900 A.D.) reveal **no significant differences**.

- **God's Promises** at Isaiah 40:8, Matthew 5:18 and 24:35 that His Word will remain.

To The Glory of God Alone

"*Soli Deo Gloria*" which is Latin for "**To the Glory of God Alone**" is an essential teaching of the Christian faith that Mormonism distorts. Christians live for the "Glory of God Alone," and not for building themselves up or exalting their own kingdoms as Mormonism teaches.

The Apostle Paul said at *Galatians 6:14*, "**...may it never be that I would boast, except in the cross of our Lord Jesus Christ...**" Yet, Joseph Smith, the founder of Mormonism, boasted that he did more than Jesus.

Joseph Smith said, "**I have more to boast of than ever any man had**. I am the only man that has ever been able to keep a whole church together... Neither Paul, John, Peter, **nor Jesus** ever did it. I **boast** that **no man** ever did such a work as I. The followers of **Jesus ran away from Him**; but the Latter-day Saints never ran away from me yet."[1]

Not only did Joseph Smith boast in himself over Christ, he told his Mormon followers in his King Follett Sermon that "God...was once a man like us" and that the goal of eternal life is "**to learn how to be gods yourselves**... by going... **from exaltation to exaltation**, until you... sit in glory... ."

Given the blasphemous teachings of Mormonism that reduce God to man in order to exalt man to

[1] *History of the Church,* May 26, 1844, Vol. 6, pp. 408-409.

the position of God, is it any wonder that Mormons "laud" Joseph Smith by singing a hymn entitled, **"Praise to the Man"** which "hails" him as "the Prophet [who] ascended to heaven [and is] **Mingling with Gods**"?

Far from giving Glory to God Alone, Mormonism exalts man in its worship services and cannot be considered Christian.

ADDITIONAL THOUGHTS:

The Mormon concept of men exalting to become gods of their own planets is a teaching that the Mormon Church has been working to try to conceal, in recent years, with statements like, "few Latter-day Saints would identify with caricatures of having their own planet... ."[2]. Yet, prior Mormon prophets had no trouble describing their dreams of becoming gods and inheriting their own planets. A 1975 Mormon Church *Ensign* publication explains: "Brethren, 225,000 of you are here tonight. I suppose 225,000 of you may **become gods**. There seems to be plenty of space out there in the universe. And the Lord has proved that he knows how to do it. I think he could make, or probably have us help make, **worlds for all of us**, for every one of us 225,000."[3]

[2] LDS.org Gospel Topic Essay, "Becoming Like God," published 2014.
[3] Spencer W. Kimball, "The Privilege of Holding the Priesthood," *Ensign,* Conference Edition, November 1975, p. 80.

Counting the Cost

Quite often when we are presenting the problems of Mormonism to an active member of the LDS Church, we find that they are not really asking if the evidence we are presenting is true but whether or not they are willing to risk losing their family, job or spouse over this information."

Because Mormonism is a culture of its own, leaving the Mormon Church often has a significant cost attached to it that may seem to outweigh the benefits of leaving for the truth.

If you find yourself in that place, we want you to consider what we have found in our journey out of Mormonism even though it has cost us nearly everything in our relationship with some of our adult children.

Jesus said in **Matthew 10:37**, **"He that loveth father or mother more than me is not worthy of me**: and he that loveth son or daughter more than me is not worthy of me."

When it comes to the possibility of losing your family, we know that it is hard to hear, but a relationship with Jesus is worth far more than any family relationship. And that comes from a heart-broken mother and father who dearly miss our relationship with some of our children and grandchildren.

When we were Mormon, we could never be sure we had done enough to be saved.

Within the Book of Mormon in **2 Nephi 25:23** it says, "...for we know that it is by grace we have been saved, **after all we can do.**" This scripture had been so ingrained into our minds that we truly believed that we had to work our way to heaven! We did not realize that grace was a free gift from God, and that all we had to do to receive it was to just believe in Jesus Christ Alone!

So at what point can any Mormon be sure he has done all he can do for salvation? **Doctrine and Covenants, Section 82:7** says, "go your ways and **sin no more**; but **unto that soul who sinneth shall the former sins return**, saith the Lord your God."

So if repeating one sin can bring back the former sins, how can any Mormon be assured of forgiveness and salvation?

Again, the works-based religion of Mormonism is the exact opposite of the biblical grace-based salvation offered in Christ who removes our sins "as far as the east is from the west" (Psalm 103:12).[1]

---

[1] See also Ephesians 2:8-9; John 5:24; Romans 8:1.

CHAPTER SIX:

YOU ARE NOT ALONE!

"Coming out of Mormonism was the single most significant, emotional and spiritual event that we had ever gone through. We felt ALONE! We did not realize that there were thousands of Mormons who had left Mormonism after they had discovered that the Mormon Church was not what we had been taught it was. We hope that our testimony and the testimonies of others we are sharing with you here will help you know that you are not alone!"

—Former Mormon Bishop Lee and Kathy Baker

YOU ARE NOT ALONE!

The Testimony of Lee and Kathy Baker

My wife Kathy and I have spent many years in various Leadership positions of the Church of Jesus Christ of Latter-day Saints. As a retired Military Intelligence Officer, I found that the key principles of authority and organization within the Mormon Church provided me with a degree of confidence. I was ordained a Mormon High Priest by Charles P. Warnick, who was ordained by the former Prophet, Thomas S. Monson.

MELCHIZEDEK PRIESTHOOD ORDINATION CERTIFICATE

This certifies that **LEE BARRY BAKER**

was ordained to the office of **HIGH PRIEST** in the Melchizedek Priesthood

in The Church of Jesus Christ of Latter-day Saints   17 MAY 19 87

by **CHARLES P. WARNICK**   whose priesthood office is   **HIGH PRIEST**

SIERRA VISTA 4TH
Ward/Branch
Sierra Vista Arizona
Stake/Mission

THE CHURCH OF
JESUS CHRIST
OF LATTER-DAY
SAINTS

Stake/Mission president (District president where authorized)

This relatively short **"Priesthood Authority Line"** was also a source of confidence and pride.

THE CHURCH OF
JESUS CHRIST
OF LATTER-DAY
SAINTS

Priesthood Authority Line

Historical Department, Member Services
50 East North Temple Street
Salt Lake City, Utah 84150

Name	Was ordained	On
By Lee Barry Baker	Who was ordained a High Priest	On May 17, 1987
By Charles Peter Warnick	Who was ordained a High Priest	On September 12, 1976
By Thomas S. Monson	Who was ordained an Apostle	On October 10, 1963
By Joseph Fielding Smith	Who was ordained an Apostle	On April 7, 1910
By Joseph F. Smith	Who was ordained an Apostle	On July 1, 1866
By Brigham Young	Who was ordained (see below)	On

Brigham Young was ordained an Apostle on 14 February, 1835 under the hands of the Three Witnesses - Oliver Cowdery, David Whitmer, and Martin Harris (see Joseph Smith, *History of the Church of Jesus Christ of Latter-Day Saints*, vol. 2, P. 187)

The Three Witnesses were called by revelation to choose the Twelve Apostles, and on 14 February, 1835 were "blessed by the laying on of hands of the Presidency,"- Joseph Smith Jr., Sidney Rigdon, and Frederick G. Williams - to ordain the Twelve Apostles (see *History of the Church*, vol. 2, Pp 185-189)

Joseph Smith, Jr., and Oliver Cowdery received the Melchizedek Priesthood in 1829 under the hands of Peter, James, and John (see *History of the Church*, vol. I, pp. 40-41).

Peter, James and John were ordained Apostles by the Lord Jesus Christ (see John 15:16)

PFJ189164 3.87   Printed in USA

As a member of the Mormon faith for 32 years, I have honorably held many Leadership positions at the Branch, Ward and Stake level. The most demanding of these "callings" was as the Bishop of the Mililani Second Ward, Mililani Stake in Hawaii. The most rewarding position was with my wife as the Young Single Adult (YSA) Leaders, of the Columbia Maryland Stake. Our YSA youth group (those unmarried between 18-30) drew its membership from as far north as Baltimore and south to Washington D.C.

As a Bishop and an Assistant Institute Instructor, I was more sensitive than others to the written history of the Church and the subjects of polygamy and polyandry. When sensitive or delicate questions were presented to us from the Mormon and non-Mormon young adults, I pledged my utmost support. Often the Christian visitors to our group knew more facts specific to the distinctively Mormon doctrine than we did, although the majority of these valid subjects would be considered as anti-Mormon.

In December of 2008, I forced my own excommunication after several painful years of meetings and letters to the highest levels of the Mormon Church concerning these questions of doctrine and history that began with the young adult singles group. As an active Mormon High Priest and Ordained Bishop, I was asked and then warned to simply leave the Church without forcing any administrative or disciplinary action as a result of my questions.

The comprehensive story of the full compilation of questions and the heart wrenching process of departing from such a controlling religious faction is detailed in my book **Mormonism: A Life Under False Pretenses – The True Story of a Mormon Bishop's Journey of Discovery** available at amazon.com.

Since my wife and I left Mormonism, we have come to know the Lord Jesus Christ. He had placed before my wife and I, five years of spiritual and emotional trials as we worked through the process of leaving Mormonism, so that we may better know His grace.

The most enlightening and rewarding action a member of the Mormon faith can do is precisely what they have been told to do, "Study the Restored Gospel of Jesus Christ and the teachings of the Prophets of the Restoration" and compare these with the teachings of the Bible and the facts of history.

From my personal family experience, one of the most dangerous elements of coming to know that the LDS Church is false, and certainly the most treacherous long-term effect of this knowledge, is the thought that *"If I was wrong about the LDS faith, is it possible that I have also been deceived by Christianity itself?"* I know that discouraging and depressing fear well from considering that as I had been so thoroughly deceived, maybe I encouraged the deception by my own deep desire for it to be true.

When one leaves the LDS Church, based on a confident witness that the very doctrine of that Church is not in harmony with the teachings of Jesus Christ, that realization and the action that one takes on behalf of that commitment, is only the first step to a closer, more personal (and certainly a more correct), relationship with Jesus Christ.

Exposing the malice in Mormonism is not the verification that Christianity itself is wrong, only that the Mormon's distorted version of Christianity is wrong. In fact, it is the exceptionally tender and legitimate teachings of Christ Himself that will expose the enormous errors.

These very teachings, chief among them: **His atonement for us**, not Brigham Young's teaching of blood atonement, **His Grace**, and not the good works of the Mormon pioneers, that stand as the example of His divine mission on our behalf.

The fact remains that if we, as former Mormons, were blinded for a time and yet remained believers in Him, then **we have lost nothing, for He never left us and we never left Him**. His guidance for us was only momentarily distorted by the teachings of Mormonism.

To my former Mormon Brothers and Sisters, my testimony is this: That **Jesus is the Christ** and that we need **not worship Him from behind** the **dark shadows** of men who would have us believe that He is the author of polygamy, polyandry, blood atonement, Lying for the Lord, or a myriad of other personally motivated corruptions. **He wants a direct and very personal relationship with each of us**, as He has ransomed our sins; not through a maze of changing doctrines or through the endless layers of administrative officers and clerks or executive church officials, committees, counsels or presidencies. **He wants us to truly know Him!**

The Testimony of Bev Wilhelm

My Mormon heritage goes all the way back to Joseph Smith. My genealogy crosses his genealogy. My beginnings were in a small town in Idaho. I went to church in an old stone building across the street from my house. Sundays were fun hearing stories about Jesus and getting a gold star on my forehead. We had a big family and lots of friends, all Mormon. I have fond memories of friendships and social gatherings.

When I was about six years old, I was with my Grandmother Lucy in the basement of that old Mormon Church in Rigby, Idaho. Grandma was talking to another woman about Jesus Christ. I wanted to know more and kept bugging her with questions. She took the time to tell me about Jesus dying on the cross for all of our sins and if we pray to Him and thank Him for His gift, He will be the constant friend by our side and we can live in heaven.

I went to another room all by myself and prayed to Jesus for his gift of salvation and Jesus has been my constant companion ever since.

As a child in the Mormon Church, all I wanted was to hear stories about Jesus. As I got older, I felt a conflict with the Jesus I knew and the Mormon teachings I grew up with. However, I did not know anything else but Mormonism, and I did not know where to go.

The Mormon Church taught that if you were not a Mormon you would not live with God in heaven. "No!" I said to this teaching. "A church and all its rules and regulations cannot get you to heaven. Jesus already did that on the cross at Calvary." I came to the conclusion that all the interviews I had from the Church to check on my worthiness was not of God, it was of man. God is my daily interviewer. Everything from the Mormon Church was man intervening between God and me.

Beginning in High School and my two years at Ricks College, I began to ask some serious questions about Mormonism. No one could answer my questions in a way that seemed right, and I was told by the Mormon Church that I did not have enough "faith." These are only a few of the questions I had:

1. If this is our probation time on earth and Jesus is our brother, and we are working to be "Gods," how can Jesus have been God when He came to earth? Wouldn't He have been in His probation on earth, just like we are?

2. I wanted to visit places mentioned in the Book of Mormon, but I was told no one knows where these places are and that there are no remnants to show where those people actually lived. When we have ample evidence of places mentioned in the Bible, it did not make sense that not even one of the Book of Mormon places could be found today. How could so many people live without leaving something behind?

3. The Bible says that God will not let His Church be taken from the earth.[1] Why, then, did the Mormon Church need to bring God's Church back?

4. At Matthew 24:35, God promised to preserve His Word. He would never let it become corrupt. I was told that the Bible was "translated" wrong by men. This was impossible in my mind, because I firmly believed God was more powerful than a man and that He would make sure His Words were what He wanted me to know.

---

[1] See Matthew 16:18 and Hebrews 12:28.

5. I wondered why it seemed to me that the Mormon Church targeted only the good people. Why don't we go out and teach all people, even if they are bad people, like in prisons? Bad people need to hear about Jesus too.[2]

6. The Bible tells me I "have" eternal life with God (1 John 5:11-13). The Mormon doctrine says I have a list of things I have to do to be able to live with God. So why, in Mormon doctrine, do I need Jesus, if I have to do things to get to heaven? Was His blood not sufficient enough to make me acceptable to God?

7. After going to the temple I told my husband, mother and father that I did not want to become a "god." They replied that I would understand and accept this teaching "in time." When I firmly stated I would not live with my husband in Heaven if I had to share him with lots of other wives, I was told I could choose whether I wanted to follow that command. But this only made me have more questions. If I could choose about this command, how many other commands could I choose to obey or not to obey?

---

[2] It is true that the LDS Church has programs for prisoners, but from my personal experience in Mormonism, it seemed that they targeted more of the good people in the areas where I lived, than they did the bad people.

Sometimes when I was given answers to questions, I found out that their answers were not reliable. For a great deal of time, I was branded a "troublemaker," "rebellious," and "faithless."

For most of my life, I have felt out of place on this earth. I know I feel this way because earth is not my home. God has a plan. He created the earth as a temporary home. Also, for most of my life I was living in a belief system that did not match with the teachings of Jesus in the Bible. I was tormented with these conflicts for 40 years.

Then, one Sunday morning in 1986, a power stronger than myself assisted me. As my family was getting ready for the LDS Church, I announced I was not going to Church. I felt a strength I had not ever experienced. I was asked if I was sick or if someone hurt my feelings? My reply was "no" to all questions.

I announced with power and affirmation, "I am not going to Church today, and I probably will not go to Church ever again." My family was in shock as they went off to the LDS Church. My two oldest sons were preparing for their missions at that time.

For 3.5 hours that day while my family was at Church, I prayed asking God to show me where He wanted me to go now? I did not know where I was going, but I trusted God to get me there.

I stepped away and just immersed myself in a quest to find the Jesus I knew as a child.

Jesus took me into the wilderness with just Him and me. He must have known it would take a long time to remove all the years of wrong teaching in the Mormon Church that I had in my head. I did not attend any church for a while. I did not want another religion to dominate my life and thoughts.

After long hours of prayer and time with Jesus, I attended a good Bible-based non-denominational Christian church in my area. The music was loud and I was standing and singing. I heard someone call my name as if it was the only sound in the room. I turned around to search out the voice. I saw no one. I still was uncertain where God wanted me, but I continued reading the Bible and visiting Christian churches. Eventually, this non-denominational church where I first heard God's voice calling me became my home church.

I'll never forget the day I was re-baptized in this new church, as a real Bible-believing Christian, and not as a Mormon.

I walked up to the water with Jesus, not just beside Me, but inside me! The water rushed over me. It was amazing! It felt like the water washed me clean of all the pain of searching for the Jesus my Grandmother had shown me.

Eventually, my husband, Woody, joined me at this Christian church. For sometime, he listened to the sermons and questioned everything the pastor taught. There were many times that he went to the leaders of our church to discuss the conflicts he had with what they were teaching and what he was taught as a Mormon. But eventually Jesus took hold of his heart and he too renounced Mormonism and embraced Christianity as taught in the Bible.

A few years ago, he started taking classes at a Bible seminary and then we moved to a new area to serve at a small church where was called to serve as an Associate Pastor.

On earth, we have a chance to know Jesus. He came to earth and gave us a gift, an awesome gift! He gave us the path to our eternal home. When Jesus died on a cross, He took with Him all of our sins, sorrows, and earthly iniquities. He did this for me and He did this for you!

What sorrow and pain he must have felt because of our sin! For a brief time, our sins separated Him from Heavenly Father. How horrible could that have been? We probably can't comprehend such a thing. We need to release our sin to Jesus and thank Him for His free gift of grace that He gave us on the cross and ask Him to take us to heaven.

It is not about me. God says my good works are like filthy rags (Isaiah 64:6). It's about Jesus and the gift of His righteousness covering my sin.

My journey is amazing! No one can take you by the hand and show you the way except Jesus. Relationship —not religion— relationship with the Lord is the way to eternal life with God!

BEV AND WOODY WILHELM

Summer of 2016

The Testimony of
Phillip and Cheryl Naugle

I was born to parents who had converted to the Church of Jesus Christ of Latter-day Saints. I was raised as a Mormon in a non-Mormon environment in rural Kansas. This presented many challenges including the exclusion from most activities that were not comprised of Mormon participants. I was thoroughly rehearsed in the mantra of defending the Church, its doctrines, and its leaders long before my mandatory baptism at age eight. I was never given the opportunity to compare my beliefs with other beliefs or to investigate other viewpoints. I was taught to "know" these things were "true,"

because it was the prescribed process of indoctrination, now referred to by neuroscientists and psychological experts as "brainwashing" or "mind control."

I was blessed with an inquisitive mind and had read all of the Standard Works of the Church (LDS four books of Scripture) by the time I was twelve years old. By age thirteen, cracks were beginning to appear regarding the veracity of what I was reading and hearing. **I wrote a letter to the Prophet of the Church requesting clarification of the Church's racial position involving blacks and the priesthood**. The reply I received from a staffer of the Prophet ignited a life-long inquisition into the Church's history and doctrines. This has resulted in my present day position as an apostate from Mormonism and strong advocate of Christianity versus Mormonism. The reply I received from the LDS Church summarized the control that Church leadership has over its members. It read as follows:

> *"Such are the mysteries of Heaven. **You are not to question the Prophet of the Church in such dealings for he is infallible**. You belong to 'the only true Church on the face of the earth' and should be thankful enough for that. Such doubts are a result of the **lack of faith** on*

your part. Pray for additional strength and knowledge in such matters that you might know assuredly of the truth of all things as you have been instructed."

What this translates to is: DO NOT QUESTION!

I grew up in Mormonism under the control of my parents who were staunch members of the Church. However, I refused to go on a mission because my questions could never be answered to my satisfaction. I moved to Utah, was married in the Salt Lake City temple, was active in my local Ward and Stake, and held many key positions. **I was often counseled by my bishop to pray harder and study more so that I would not have questions**, especially the ones he could not answer.

As a young married man my employer transferred me to Las Vegas. I began to investigate the history of the area and its founders. I learned that Mormons discovered the place and that they currently own all or part of the brothels, casinos, and other establishments with gambling devices. Prominent Mormons held positions in the local and state government as well as positions on the gaming commission. Although I was restricted from drinking caffeine drinks, the Church owned all of the COKE distributorships in Nevada and

Utah. During my employment, I saw my former Salt Lake City bishop and other prominent Utah Mormons engage in gaming, drinking, and other illicit activities while visiting Las Vegas. **They were doing the same activities that they used to preach against when I lived in Salt Lake City**.

I went to my new Las Vegas bishop with my concerns. I truly wanted to be a good member of the Church, but I was conflicted with its irreconcilable doctrines and applications. Within a short time, I was served a subpoena from a Clark County Sheriff summoning me to a Church court to evaluate my membership credentials in the Church. I was being charged with blasphemy. I had forgotten lesson number one – DO NOT QUESTION!

I was excommunicated at that meeting which I chose not to attend at the advice of my counsel. Per the usual practice of the Church, they notified my family in Utah that I had been excommunicated. **Then, my family held a meeting where they disowned me as a member of their family.**

Years later, after losing my family, my wife and my business because of the excommunication, I moved back to my roots in Kansas and met Cheryl who is now my wife. Cheryl was a Lutheran. The only thing she knew about the LDS Church was the Mormon Tabernacle Choir she enjoyed watching on Sunday morning television. She wanted to know my story, so I told her about my life in Utah and Mormonism. Having lived her whole life within a few miles of the place of her birth, she wanted to visit Utah and help soothe tensions with my family who had abandoned me.

Instead of being dismayed, she was intrigued. She thought the people were kind and thoughtful, had high morals, and had an aura about them she could not understand. The cities were clean and there was less drinking and smoking than the environment she was used to. So she wanted to move to Utah.

When anyone moves to Utah, especially to Orem, UT (Family City USA), that person is immediately asked if he is a member of the Church. You do not have to guess which Church they are asking about. If you are not a member, you are encouraged to allow the LDS missionaries to visit your home. Being married to a wonderful woman was important to me at that stage of my life, I was determined not to let religion mess it up again. So I consented.

Cheryl liked the eternal family idea and was hearing things about never having to worry about divorce. She had gone through one herself. We were promised that we would live longer because of our adherence to the Word of Wisdom, etc.

Within a year, we were baptized into the LDS Church. For me, it was the second time. We had to wait a year because the Church had to have the time to investigate the reasons for my excommunication. During the interim, it was painfully necessary to grovel to local Stake, District, and Salt Lake leaders of the Church. Eternal blessings that were forfeited at the time of excommunication, had to be restored and embarrassing and personal interviews had to reflect my total commitment to the Church in order to be reinstated. Once that occurred, it was still necessary to wait another year before we could be sealed in the temple "for time and all eternity."

Walla! **My family loved me again!** My brother and sisters treated me as if I had never been shunned and all acquaintances were automatically renewed. I have to admit, it was a great feeling to have my family again. I was fully active in the Church, and at one time, Cheryl and I combined held nine positions in our local Ward and Stake.

During my tenure as a Sunday school teacher of 10-year olds, I attended Sharing Time with my class. During the proceeding, the children were asked to stand and salute with their Scriptures shouting "Scripture Power." All of my questions regarding the Church came back to me in a flash. I had an immediate headache and excused myself to go home. When Cheryl arrived, she wanted to know why I left so hurriedly and did not stay for Sacrament meeting. I told her the last time I saw anything like the Scripture salute was with old black and white movies of the Hitler Youth Movement.

I continued to go to Church with her and the kids but would take a yellow pad with me and draw a line down the middle, writing "Christ" above one half and "Joseph Smith" above the other. I would tally according to what I heard during the meeting. Jesus always lost by about 20-1.

Cheryl and I fought about the Church. I bought her a small mail and copy store to get her out of the house, and I went to work. As a private investigator by profession, I knew how to research. For the next five years, every waking moment was spent researching the Church, its history, its leaders, and its doctrine. The Internet was a fantastic tool of information never before available. I built enough courage and knowledge in five years to confront Cheryl with my findings. One evening before bedtime, I knelt beside the bed, took her by the hand and said:

"Honey, you know I love you more than

YOU ARE NOT ALONE!

anything in this world. I have something to tell you."

She thought I was going to confess to an affair and later said she wished I had. I told her of the research I had been doing and the results I had found. I told her the Church was not as it claimed, and that Joseph Smith was a liar, a pedophile, a polygamist, a bigamist, a murderer, and a member of the occult. He was certainly not a martyr. I further explained that leaders of the Church today had the same information, but continued to exploit its members for financial gain.

A year and a half later, after thousands of arguments and late night discussions, and much prayer, Cheryl finally understood what I was going through. **For me to accept Mormonism as a fraud, the "god" I had prayed to for wisdom and strength, for my family, for safety, for healing – that "god" had to die!** I had to realize the "god" of Mormonism was a false "god." This was no easy task. It would be necessary for me to process this trauma by first denying the existence of any "god." I know many who leave the Church after much study and prayer who have experienced the same feelings. Gradually, common sense took over when I began to realize the Mormon "god" was merely an exalted man who is not the

Supreme Uncreated God of the Bible—this false "god" of Mormonism had to cease to exist!

Cheryl realized my emotions and logic were in conflict with what I had been taught my whole life and what I was now learning by studying outside of the Church's sources of information. I felt the Church had messed with my soul and had polluted my mind! I was not a naïve individual. I was not an unlearned individual. I was not an uneducated individual. How could I have let this happen to me?

I was a high school baseball coach in the area. One of my players was the son of a pastor of a small evangelical Church. Cheryl called him up and asked when his services were. We attended the next Sunday and sat in the back row dressed like Mormons. It was readily apparent we were new when a couple of hundred filed past us dressed in shorts, halter tops, sandals, and jeans carrying Big Gulps and coffee. We would have never been able to attend a Mormon Church dressed like that!

Then the music started – drums, guitars, electric piano. Wow! Nothing like the dirge music we were used to. Then the words of the song came up on the wall. *"God Is An Awesome God."* Tears flooded my eyes. After several other songs, which only intensified what I was feeling, the pastor stood and caught my eye saying, "...**it**

is not the religion that counts, but your relationship with Christ..." Cheryl still remembers me elbowing her in the ribs as my eyes said, "I told you so."

We were lovingly accepted into that small Christian setting. I was soon asked to teach classes on Mormonism versus Christianity. We were able to bring dozens of people out of Mormonism and help families who had lost members to the LDS Church.

When my youngest son was appointed to the Air Force Academy in Colorado Springs, we took the opportunity to move out of what Mormons consider "God's Country" (that is, Utah). Since that time, we have dedicated our lives to helping Mormons in transition to Christianity, and in educating Christian pastors and congregations, small groups and Sunday school classes on the topic of what goes on "inside Mormonism." So far, we have spoken to Focus on the Family and other global ministry organizations, and have been well received wherever we go.

I was involved in the Mormon Church as an active temple going member for 50 years. Cheryl was involved for 15 years. It was easier for her to leave Mormonism because she had been raised Lutheran and knew who Jesus was. She had simply ignored the Mormon "god" who was replaced in her mind by the Jesus she grew up with. She had embraced Mormonism for all the obvious reasons: high morals, family values, clean living, eternal families, peer and social acceptance, etc. The doctrine of the Church was secondary.

I on the other hand had always tried to live my religion even though I had doubts about it. I remember my continuous prayer from my youth was for wisdom and the ability to decipher good from evil. **Establishing a relationship with Jesus Christ has been a life long journey for me and did not happen in a flash of light or clap of thunder. I believe my efforts to find the truth finally enabled me to see the truth.**

I had attended the LDS Church every Sunday my entire youth until one Sunday as a high school senior, I was asked by my girlfriend to attend the Presbyterian Church with her. I remember very distinctly the service that day as the life of Jesus was being preached from the pulpit. It was something different from what I was used to hearing in the LDS Church and a special feeling came over me that I never forgot for over 30 years. That feeling came back and I recognized it as such when I attended that small Evangelical Free Church for the first time in Utah. That was confirmation to me that I was doing the right thing by leaving the Mormon Church. I recognized the hand of the Savior that day in what was happening to me.

I am now fully committed to helping members of the LDS Church answer questions they have regarding their faith and how they can establish a relationship with Jesus Christ—this relationship has been forbidden by LDS Church authority Bruce R. McConkie in an address to the BYU devotional audience in 1987, but **this relationship with Jesus Christ is what Christianity is all about!**

The Testimony of Rob and Laura Butterfield

I (Rob) was born into an LDS home and raised in Salt Lake City, Utah. In my teenage years, I became disillusioned by the inconsistencies I found within the LDS Church. For many years, I believed that I didn't need God in my life, but yet I still considered myself a Mormon. Finally, my search for the truth about God and what He has to offer led me to the REAL Jesus of the Bible. After I accepted the Lord, I was able to help lead Laura (my future wife at the time) to the Lord.

I (Laura) was born as a Navajo Indian and raised in an LDS foster family in Utah. As a Mormon, I was proud of my heritage as a "Lamanite" descendant of *Book of Mormon* people. But as a young adult, I fell away because I was unable to live up to all of the Church's standards. "No one can be that perfect!" I thought.

Then I started dating Rob who was an Ex-Mormon. He too had been raised LDS, but had come to know the REAL Jesus of the Bible.

We dated and were engaged within two months, but only to embark on a difficult journey of different faiths. By summer, we ended the relationship. In September 2000, I took a new job in New Jersey. A week before leaving, I got a card in the mail from Rob. He expressed his desire that he only wanted to share the true Jesus with me and that I can have a personal relationship with Jesus like he did. I called him and we debated that issue right up to the time I left for New Jersey.

While I was in New Jersey, I really started to have doubts about the Mormon Church. Not to mention the fact that Rob continued to call and share with me about the true Jesus of the Bible. I prayed, read the Bible, the Book of Mormon, the Doctrine and Covenants searching for the truth. My soul was literally on the edge of heaven or hell. I needed to know the truth!

I started attending Calvary Hope Church, and I tuned into the local radio station and started listening to Christian pastors. I wondered how these pastors knew God's truth and I didn't. How could this be so easy for everyone else but me? Why was I struggling to know the truth?

Then on October 23, 2000, I went to the local library and downstairs of the library where I found books about Ex-Mormons who had come out of the LDS Church. I also found books that exposed many of the problems with the LDS Church. I read them until I was sick to my stomach because God was revealing the evil of the Mormon Church to me. I also felt an evil presence surround me and finally I had to get out of the library.

I was driving my rental car crying, scared and shaken by this experience when a Christian pastor on the radio announced how to receive the gift of salvation. I pulled over into a theater parking lot and called my sister-in-law Audra who had just accepted the real Lord Jesus into her life one year earlier. She answered the phone and tearfully led me in the sinner's prayer to receive the Lord into my life.

The very instant I accepted Jesus into my heart, the fear I had been experiencing immediately left me and was replaced with total peace that only my Savior could give me! I left a message on Rob's answer machine saying, *"I am a new creature!"* When he got my message, he replied, *"It's about time!"*

"He that hath received his testimony hath set to his seal that God is true." --John 3:33

The Testimony of Chuck Matteson

My wife and I were lifelong members in the LDS Church. We were sealed in the Seattle temple for all time and eternity as husband and wife. It wasn't long and we were on our way to raising a family of five children of our own.

Our family's eternal salvation depended on our ability to perform and meet all obligations required and expected by the Church. So we all pressed on, putting on that Sunday face that hides the real feelings we possess from wear and tear, over extending ourselves in callings to serve, and over-committing additional time that will eventually lead to mindless insanity. Is this truly God's plan for happiness?

As years go by, the standard mind thought is cemented in every LDS worker bee, to bring to pass the glory of God, building up His Church, and the establishment of Zion. **Imagine! We were a part of this glorious venture, and in**

**return, we are assured a place in the
eternities with our families and loved ones.
Not a bad trade, eh?** How blessed we were as
long as we never questioned anything, or
challenged the Church's history or early
beginnings. **Think about it... Why have no
artifacts EVER been discovered that coincide
with the Book of Mormon story? It's simple...
It never happened!** No mega wars, no jumbo
civilizations, no elephants here, no nothing. This
is a truth that cannot be hidden, but LDS people
won't stop and think about that, will they? The
Mormon folk are taught repetitiously and
continue to sing over and over that if they'll only
believe and follow the prophet, no thinking
needs be done, as it has been done for them.

After all, we thought it would be detrimental to
the establishment of God if anything taught as
truth were exposed as an untruth. How
fortunate we were to have a living Latter-day
Prophet to lead, guide and direct the affairs of
the Church and further explain the mysteries of
the Kingdom. If we do as we're directed, we were
taught that our place in the Celestial Kingdom is
made sure. The eternities will be a place of
peace, joy, and security of being with our
families and loved ones. How beautiful!

And it came to pass, **after admitting to myself
that something is wrong** with the Church, its
beginnings, and the very nature of its self-
proclaimed supreme authority on the earth, that
**we officially dismissed ourselves and
removed our names from the Church records**.

By voluntarily opting out of the Church program, we no longer had to struggle with the guilt of not meeting "Church" expectations. No more mandatory tithing for admission to the temple to receive God's blessings, no money...no eternal blessings folks. No more guilt for not accepting callings to voluntarily serve within the local wards or stake and sustain the steady progression towards religious dominance in the community "for the glory of God". No more guilt. No more insanity!

Since our pulling back from the LDS Church, we both as well as our children have noticed a peaceful and calming within our souls. Seriously, a great calming and peace of mind. **It's hard to explain the relief we now feel, except we understand that truth does bring peace and joy.** We now have a divine purpose within our religious beliefs. The word "ministry" has taken on a whole new and exciting meaning.

Serving others out of joy, now comes from the heart. The teachings of Christ and the biblical apostles now make more sense to us. We no longer pick up an LDS publication or doctrinal book for confusing questions concerning the gospel. Why? Again, the answer is simple.

It was the Mormon faith and its teachings that complicated an uncomplicated gospel. It was Mormon teachings that frustrate Christ's intent for our lives and has scrambled His message for mankind. It is due to the teachings of the Mormon faith that have required further explanation of principles, rites, and authority that prompt constant encouragement to subscribe to their periodicals, update yourselves on current prophesies, and continue your doctrinal indoctrination.

An LDS person is flooded with direction that is unfortunately interpreted as true gospel, rather than a true gospel fact. **Please know that the gospel of Christ was meant to serve man, and man to serve one another. Unscramble your minds if you can, and realize that God was never the author of confusion. His message is simple.** It is by man that it has been overblown, and become so complex. You do not need a myriad of LDS doctrine books to understand what God wants from you. Christ spoke plain, and so did His Apostles.

Who is right? Christ or the LDS Church? You must choose whom you will serve. Thing is, you do have a choice. For us, we chose freedom from guilt. We chose joy for our family. We chose to understand what ministering to others truly means. Christ's love was for the people. He truly loved us and endured the clutches of death on our behalf. **You must learn to trust in Him, and love Him all over again**. Look up and wonder if God was the author of such confusion and burden. He is not! I urge you to save your life and the life blood of your family. Get out while you still have a mind left to do so.

In Jesus' name, Be blessed. Chuck

CHAPTER SEVEN:

LEAVING MORMONISM WITHOUT LOSING YOUR FAITH

"Since we've left the Mormon Church, the depth of our understanding of the true message of the Bible has brought us a lasting freedom and peace, never before experienced, even as an active Bishop of the Mormon Church. We successfully left our faith in Mormonism without losing our faith in Jesus Christ. This new and very personal relationship with Jesus Christ awaits you, when you move on the inspiration of the Holy Spirit of God to guide you as you search for the Truth."

—Former Mormon
Bishop Lee and Kathy Baker

After Mormonism, What?
~ Chuck Matteson's Experience

You may be asking: "So What Do I Do Now?" You have finally broken free from the "herd" of Mormonism, but you feel hopelessly lost and without direction now...

HOW DID YOU GET HERE?

In the LDS Church, you were told what to think, where to go, what to do, and how to do it. You had your *Church Handbook* that was approved by the Presidency of the Church for your study and spiritual edification. You maintained faith with the Brethren and local leaders of the Church.

You had been told to simply follow the Prophet and everything will be made sure. You carried a membership card that got you into the temple. You passed your exams with the local Bishop, the Stake President, and anyone else who had been proclaimed to be an authority over you. You memorized all the songs since primary, memorized a few Scriptures from the *Book of Mormon*, dressed like everyone else in the Church, spoke like everyone else, served without reservations like everyone else. **You were in fact, a living clone of everyone else in Mormonism.**

LEAVING MORMONISM WITHOUT LOSING YOUR FAITH

You knew what time your assigned meeting schedules were and stressed the importance of being there on time in your Sunday best as you scurried about to get your preferred seat in the Chapel. You knew where the Church House was located, what Ward your were assigned to and who your Stake President was. **You never had to think about what you were doing, because you were doing what everyone else seemed to be doing**.

You were not alone. You thought there was safety in numbers. You were officially one of the "herd." You wanted what everyone else was wanting, which was an assurance that God loved you and your family and that He had a place for you in the eternities. You felt that your near insanity from hours of countless stewardship assignments was evidence that you were doing all that you could to assure yourself of a place in the Celestial Kingdom with God. Am I right on this?

WHAT ARE YOU GOING TO DO NOW?

This is going to be fun folks. Now, that you have chosen to be free from the mindless tasks that encumbered so much of your time, what are you going to do now that you have stepped off the train? You no longer are choosing to be a Mormon worker-bee, running mindlessly from meeting-to-meeting, task-to-task, event-to-event.

You have been kept so busy that you have never been really free to think for yourself and to truly commune with God as He has intended. There is no one telling you what to do now, no one calling you on the phone, no one from the Bishopric stopping by to give you another calling, no more Home teachers or visiting teachers with cupcakes. Nothing! You are going to have to make your own cupcakes now.

YOU ARE FREE TO...

You now are free to think; you are free to act responsibly, and you are free to walk with Christ as His gospel was intended for you. **This new feeling of freedom may be a little scary to some**; yet eagerly embraced by others. Your heart feels free, but your mind and years of weekly habits may insanely be driving you to feel compelled to get ready for the next meeting, but there are no more meetings now. There are no men claiming "priesthood authority" over your life and aggressively advising you of what not to do, or reminding you of your responsibility in your Church "calling," and no more tireless guilt trips.

You may struggle accepting the fact that you have permission to think for yourself again. However, **God gave you a mind, and now you finally get to use it**. You are now free to commune with God on a more personal level, and to seek the work He intended for you, **without someone telling you that you have been "duly called" to serve in whatever capacity they think is best for you.** The authority kick is now gone. **There is only you and God. Do you get it? Just you and God!**

It is now all about your relationship with Jesus! It is the basic foundational understanding of **Who** Christ is, **what He has done for you**, what He **means to you,** and what **He truly wants for you,** that will set your spirit free!

> *"And you will **know the truth**, and the **truth will make you free**... So if the **Son makes you free**, you will be **free indeed**."—John 8:32, 36 (NASB - New American Standard Bible)*

Get rid of the Standard Works "Scripture" offered through the LDS Church. Consider getting rid of your *King James Version* of the Bible and purchasing a modern translation, like the *New King James Version*, or BETTER yet, the *New American Standard Bible* or the *New International Version*. Reading the Bible in your current language will be refreshing for you, because for the first time, you will begin to understand what the Bible is actually saying.

Remember, there is nothing special in the archaic language of the King James Bible.

Nobody speaks that way anymore, and God certainly doesn't regard those who talk that way in their prayers as more holy than those who speak in modern English.

So, I recommend that you get a Bible that you can actually read and understand. Then, over time, you will begin to know what Christ's message truly is and how it applies to your life.

YOU ARE NOT GOING CRAZY!

There are so many emotions an Ex-Mormon feels when he or she steps off the treadmill of Mormonism. **Feelings of betrayal, anger, distrust, fear, depression and confusion are just the beginning of a list that could go on and on.** Yet, every person who begins to think for himself—as God intended the creative human mind to do—will begin to experience a sense of freedom and a feeling of being lost, without direction at the same time.

God has been waiting for you to open your eyes and to see life as it was meant to be. **If you feel lost, it is only because you have become used to being told how to jump, when to jump, and how high you must jump to receive your "glory" in God's Kingdom**. But aren't your legs a bit tired by now? Mine were! God never put jumping games on the earth that required people to hop through so many silly hoops to get a bit of heavenly real estate. So, stop jumping around! You no longer need to play the game "Simon Says." (A game for children where Mr. Simon tells one what to do and that person must do it perfectly in order to win).

Trust me on this; works-oriented religions, like Mormonism, are nothing but a game made by people to control as many other people as they can. Members of the LDS Church love to play a religious version of the game "Simon Says." They just don't realize that they are playing it in hopes of obtaining peer approval and spiritual points. Peer approval is silly and stressful. It has nothing to do with God's approval on your life. **Why not become approved of God by placing your full trust in the sufficient sacrifice of Jesus Christ on behalf of your sins? That's all that really matters anyway**. Do you feel better now?

*"He made Him who knew no sin **to be sin on our behalf**, so that **we might become the righteousness of God in Him**."*
—*2 Corinthians 5:21 (NASB)*

*"And may be found in Him, **not having a righteousness of my own** derived from the Law, but **that which is through faith in Christ**, the righteousness which comes from God on the basis of faith."*
—*Philippians 3:9 (NASB)*

FORGETTING THE PAST AND MOVING ON...

"...I press on so that I may lay hold of that for which also I was laid hold of by Christ Jesus. Brethren, I do not regard myself as having laid hold of it yet; but one thing I do: forgetting what lies behind and reaching forward to what lies ahead, I press on toward the goal for the prize of the upward call of God in Christ Jesus."—Philippians 3:12-14 (NASB)

Learning how to forget what has been deeply engrained in your brain will take time, my friend. Be patient with yourself. If you have been a Mormon since childhood, the roots of what you have been told run deep, but regardless of how long you have been involved, it takes time to deprogram yourself and detach your feelings from it as well.

Remember that this Mormon mind-game was of men's doing, not God's. You were programmed to sit, smile, bear testimonies, tell your friends that families can be together forever, serve a mission, marry a missionary, go to the temple often, pay a full tithe, give a fast offering, provide community service, serve in the ward, teach, call each other "brother" and "sister," protect yourself by wearing holy garments, perform baptisms for the dead, research and put together your genealogy, remember your secret new name given in the temple, the signs and penalties and the promises associated with each one of them. Good golly! Were you stressed out? You were not alone!

Now is the time to get rid of your temple garments. If you honestly believe they will protect you, light them on fire and be grateful you weren't in them as you watch them burn; or you can borrow a gun and go shoot a hole in them.

Why do this? Because Superman never wore them, and there is no reason to falsely believe they are able to protect you. They are not magic and mysterious, and they don't stop bullets. The sacred emblems stitched on them are rather silly too. I'll prove it to you. **Look up the signs and emblems used in Free Masonry. You will find that the emblems of Mormonism are used in Masonry, and they even have similar meanings within the Masonic Lodge too!**

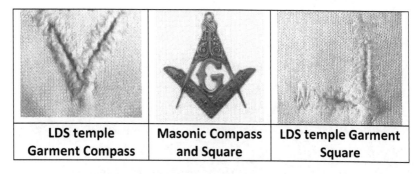

LDS temple Garment Compass	Masonic Compass and Square	LDS temple Garment Square

Do you see that Joseph Smith was influenced by Masonry? Did you know that he was himself a Mason? Oh, now your eyes are beginning to open! While we're at it, **how about those sacred handshakes** that will great you by the angels who stand as sentinels at the gates of heaven. **Well, the Masons already laid claim to those shakes too.** The problem is that the Masons have been around a lot longer than Mormons. Please don't think that God is a Mason. He is not. This was all designed by man in their secret clubs and societies to make followers believe that they are a cut above the rest. Even the language used in the temple is similar to the rights and rituals of Mormonism.

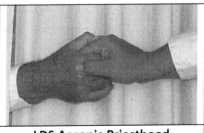

LDS Aaronic Priesthood Handshake	Masonic Handshake

As you can see, Joseph Smith wasn't very clever on his own, but was brilliant in converting the handshakes, signs and symbols of Masonry into his religious forum. Then, he attached the claim of mysterious promises from God if you joined his religious club. It worked! People ran to it as God's "sacred" secrets for mankind.

Joseph appointed himself as the Prophet for religious clout. People wore this funny underwear, memorized the script, and learned the rituals required at the veil and were internally brainwashed into believing that they had potentially earned their status as "Gods" and "Goddesses," "Priests" and "Priestesses" in Heaven, being destined to live happily ever after.

Meanwhile, Joseph enjoyed the privileges of his self-appointed authority, multiple wives, religious status and position, money, and growing real estate in the Church. He enjoyed it until folks got tired of his lies and polygamous activities and killed him.

It is absolutely unbelievable, but we got duped! Quit reading the Church's publications so you can discover for yourself that history is not what others want you to believe it was. Don't take my word for it. Do your own research of the truth and you will also see that the spiritual food Joseph Smith served is no longer delicious. Joseph was not all the Church builds him up to be. We are so happy you decided to set down your fork, and remove your napkin. Your first challenge is to stop wearing those crazy garments! There is no need to dress up in funny underwear any longer. Enjoy your freedom and be daring! Choose underwear with colors and see how you feel tomorrow. Be free at last!

FACING YOUR LDS FRIENDS...

One of the things you'll have to face is the fact that **your friends in the Church will not understand your new freedom**. They will not comprehend how you could let this perceived "eternal salvation" slip through your fingers. They will question, "**What on earth happened to your testimony?**"

You have to realize that they still are sucked up into the "happily ever after" storybook ending of Mormonism. Just forgive them and pray for God's Holy Spirit to open their eyes. Perhaps, later you will be able to help them question their beliefs and be instrumental in leading them out of the LDS rat race. For now, they'll look at you with sympathetic eyes, and wonder what has happened to you.

Don't you want to be as miserable as them? They now feel betrayed by you, as they must carry the burdens of Mormonism alone without your help. Misery loves company, and now you're not there. They simply won't allow themselves to grasp the idea that there are no real "Prophets" in the LDS Church, but only a "President" and two "Counselors" (that is, Vice Presidents) of the Church Corporation.

Think about it; when was the last time they had any significant new revelations? Their corporation has a Board of Directors called "Apostles," and various global leadership sales people like missionaries who sell Mormonism door-to-door. They all have great stories with a blind eye on one goal, to expand their organization to ensure its survival. They might as well say something like this, and just be honest about their intentions:

> *"**Everyone please continue to work for free in exchange for blessings we've arranged for you with God!** We have got connections since we are the true church. Our leaders heard it from God Himself. No more worries, just keep working at those callings as we've got a big bag of blessings in Heaven for ya!"*

That was harsh, wasn't it? I do apologize for any hurt feelings, but sometimes we need to call it like it is in order to expose their hidden agenda.

Fortunately, more and more people are seeing the truth as it is, not as "the Brethren" spin it to be. Many are leaving Mormonism to seek God as Jesus Christ prescribed in the Holy Bible.

> *"And a lawyer stood up and put Him to the test, saying, '**Teacher, what shall I do to inherit eternal life?**' And He said to him, 'What is written in the Law? How does it read to you?' And he answered, '**YOU SHALL LOVE THE LORD YOUR GOD WITH ALL YOUR HEART**, AND WITH ALL YOUR SOUL, AND WITH ALL YOUR STRENGTH, AND WITH ALL YOUR MIND; AND **YOUR NEIGHBOR AS YOURSELF**.' "—Luke 10:25-27 (NASB)*

Christ made things so simple: Love God, and love your neighbor as yourself. Now, that is not too difficult to understand, is it? People, who have ulterior motives, have mucked up His message under an "organized religion." **We all get caught up in the grandeur of something bigger and better, but God didn't need "bigger and better" to relay His message to mankind. He gave us Christ**. Now, this is your time for renewed discovery of everything Christ meant for you to have, and what God wants you to be "in Him" alone.

*"But whatever things were gain to me, those things I have counted as loss for the sake of Christ. More than that, **I count all things to be loss in view of the surpassing value of knowing Christ Jesus my Lord**, for whom I have suffered the loss of all things, and count them but rubbish in order that I may gain Christ, and may **be found in Him, not having a righteousness of my own** derived from the Law, **but that which is through faith in Christ**, the righteousness which comes from God on the basis of faith."*
— *Philippians 3:7-9 (NASB)*

Your quest is now to discover who you really are in Christ, and what you mean to others who need to see Christ through you. Now, you will gain a better understanding of what a ministry truly means, and how it applies to you.

You will find that God wants you to join Him in His work that he has already begun in you and around you.

> *"For it is **God who is at work in you**, both to will and to work for His good pleasure."*
> — *Philippians 2:13 (NASB)*

Discover the work God has for you and see where you fit in the family of Christ by visiting different Christian Churches in your area. **Find a church family that teaches the Bible verse-by-verse and supports your growth in Christ**. Don't be afraid to consider a Bible study group within your congregation. For once, you may actually learn something that makes a lot of sense, and you will see that you are not really alone after all!

So, don't worry about secret handshakes, wearing special clothes, or maintaining a certain appearance to impress people or God. Most Christians are normal people like you and me. Ties and dresses are no longer required. Jeans are okay now. I have found thongs on my feet and a pair of baggy pants appropriate on hot Sundays. No one seems to care.

People come from all walks of life and from many different circumstances. **Christ still accepts us as we are**, and He has no ridiculous expectations of you. He wants you to remember

Him and what He has done, and to live for Him each day. That's it! Someday, maybe you'll be ready to share this message with a friend, as the gospel is free to all who will receive it. Garments are not required. **So, relax! Find Christ's message and God's love all over again, and this time, for the right reasons.**

REMOVING YOUR NAME FROM THE LDS CHURCH...

When I left the Church of Jesus Christ of Latter-day Saints, I took the bold step and **asked them to remove my name from their records** and to void my membership. Do you know what happened? I actually received a letter from Salt Lake City, *finally* granting my wishes. **But they required a process**, or rather, their corporate legal hoops to jump through in order to meet my demand.

So, **I wrote my letter in a particular way** that prevented them from sending members of the Bishopric to hound my doorstep.

The good news is that I am finally free for God now! He can use me as He wishes to use me. My relationship with God has taken a new and refreshing dimension. Ah... smell that? The smog has lifted, and a fresh mountain breeze has raised my spiritual wings.

Here is something you may consider. **Someday, you may choose to be re-baptized unto Christ and to openly honor Him by renewing your faith in Him**. It is okay to recommit your life.

Think of it as washing away the old, and arising anew. Your choice to be re-baptized may offer you a "clean break" from your past. It did for me. It was my way of putting a period at the end of the LDS story. One big dot, and it was done. Free at last!

It is refreshing being a follower of Christ, and an instrument for God as He directs. **It is really all about our relationship with Him, and no one else**. You can't do better than that, my friends. No way! In leaving Mormonism and embracing the simplicity of Christ, I simply decided to cut out the middleman, and to go directly to God. You do the same and you will be amazed by Him.

Remember, you are not alone! There are Christian fellowships around you, and they will openly love you and accept you as you are. Find a church that best fits your personality, fulfills your needs, and where you can serve in freedom.

Remember, Christ accepts you as you are and true Christians will embrace you and love you with the love Christ gives.

Learn from other Christians, and share the joy you have found with others. **Let your quest for God begin with the freshness of Christ's Spirit and let Him lead you into all peace, growth and understanding**. It is a quest well worth your time that will bring eternal blessings.

You can finally relax, ponder, and pray, without outside influences on your back. It is now just you and your God. Neat thought, isn't it? Just you and God!

> " *'Come to Me, all who are weary and heavy-laden, and I will give you rest. Take My yoke upon you, and learn from Me, for I am gentle and humble in heart; and you shall find rest for your souls. For My yoke is easy, and My load is light.'* " — Matthew 11:28-30 (NASB)

So, if you have family and friends in Mormonism that have disassociated themselves from you, realize that they never have had the love of Christ in them. **Remember, you did not denounce Christ, but only omitted the static between you and God. So, be patient with them and love them with the love of Christ**.

In time, they may grow to admire your attitude toward life, your love of the gospel, and your ministry of faith that God has begun to do in and through you.

Remember, you cannot force feed anyone that wishes not to eat. **Just let them see how delicious the fruits of the real gospel truly are on your side of the fence.** One day, they may choose to eat with you, and what a glorious day for you and your loved-ones that will be!

> *"**Be anxious for nothing**, but in everything by prayer and supplication with thanksgiving let your requests be made known to God. **And the peace of God, which surpasses all comprehension, shall guard your hearts and your minds in Christ Jesus.**" —Philippians 4:6-7 (NASB)*

My friends, be blessed in Christ.

Chuck

Writing Your Resignation Letter

If you want to have your name removed from the LDS Church's membership records, you must make your letter strong and to the point. Although some may feel that this type of approach is too harsh, we have learned that if you do not make it forceful in this manner, they may delay your request and harass you as to your reasons for leaving with the hopes of getting you to change your mind.

We know it works, and anyone wanting to remove their name can use the following format and sample letter. Many people are afraid to be this stern, but it is **absolutely necessary**! Below is a copy of the cover information that one Ex-Mormon couple used to remove their names from the LDS Church's records. They testified that when they used this format:

> *"We received a response before the 30 days were up and a letter stating that our names had been removed, but they wanted to make that sure we knew what we were doing because it would jeopardize our eternal salvation, and they would be more than happy to have us return to the church. What a joke. We are happy to be free at last!"*

Please be advised that you must file a letter in writing to the **membership department** of the

Church's "confidential records" in Salt Lake City, **your Stake President**, and **your Bishop**. This should be done by typing a letter (not hand writing it), and sending copies of the same letter to all three **by Certified Mail with Return Receipt** or by **Priority Mail with Delivery Confirmation**.

It is important that you select the "Return Receipt" or the "Delivery Confirmation" option for these services to require the recipient's signature. This eliminates your chances of the LDS Church returning your letter. Address your letter to the LDS Church's records department in Salt Lake at:

**LDS Membership Records Department
50 E North temple Room 1372
Salt Lake City, UT 84150-5310**

If you don't already know the names and addresses of your Bishop and Stake President, you may obtain their information by calling the LDS Church boundaries office at: **(801) 240-3500**

When you call this number, inform the operator that you need to know who your Bishop and your Stake President are. Tell them your address (You may give them your name or use a different name; it doesn't matter. You are seldom asked, so often, you don't even have to give them your name.) Ask for the names and addresses of your

Bishop and Stake President. They will give it to you without question.

Your letter must contain the following:

1. Your name, address, and date of birth. State that you want your name and the names of your children and spouse (if applicable) removed from the records of the Church as well.

2. State that this decision is final and you wish no personal contact.

3. Emphasize that you do not want the word "excommunication" used in connection with this request. You must threaten to go to the press or ACLU or an attorney if this request is not honored.

4. Emphasize that this is to be done within 30 days.

5. Feel free to express yourself in any way regarding the Church or your new found faith. This is optional.

Talk to no one in the Church until you receive written notice of the removal of your name(s).

SAMPLE RESIGNATION LETTER
(Names, Addresses, Birth Dates, Stake and Ward information has been changed to maintain the privacy of the individuals involved.)

Luke P. Kimball
911 Scenery Drive
Smith, UT 84000

Date

DS Membership Records Department
50 E North temple Room 1372
Salt Lake City, UT 84150-5310

James Smith - Stake President
123 James Smith Street,
Smith, UT 84000

John Smith – Bishop
555 John Smith Street,
Smith, UT 84000

Dear Sirs:

We, the undersigned, do hereby request the removal of the membership records of our family from the Church of Jesus Christ of Latter Day Saints, including: Luke P. Kimball whose date of birth is 03/09/1982, Lucy R. Kimball whose date of birth is 7/15/1983, Stephen J. Kimball whose date of birth is 09/10/2005, and Susan E. Kimball whose date of birth is 06/24/2008.

We request that this request be processed immediately, as our decision is final and not subject to discussion with any representative from the Church of Jesus Christ of Latter Day Saints at any level be it ward, stake or otherwise.

We are voluntarily leaving the LDS church and demand that the term "excommunication" not be used in any correspondence concerning this matter. Our family does not wish to be the subject of any controversy, conversation or innuendo among the members of the Canyon Valley Second Ward or other companion wards which constitute the Provo Canyon Valley Stake of the LDS church. The source of any controversy, conversation or innuendo can easily be identified because this notice is being sent only to those who have direct charge of our records. Violation of this confidentiality will be appropriately dealt with.

Be it hereby known that we are not resigning our membership because of any "sin" on our part as is commonly alleged when persons leave the church. Nor are we resigning our membership because of the actions of any member(s) of the Provo Canyon Valley Stake or more particular, the Canyon Valley Second Ward. Furthermore, we are not resigning our membership due to any personality conflicts or human relationships.

We ask only that you honor our request immediately and that we receive written indication from the Salt Lake membership department verifying compliance with our request. We know that this should not take more than 30 days. We know it to be a common practice for Church leaders to procrastinate requests of this nature. We urge you not to do so and again reiterate that this is our final decision and not subject to discussion. Once we have received verification that our names have been removed from the records of the church you may continue the warm and congenial relationships to which we are accustomed.

However, you should be aware that in order to protect the integrity of our family, it would be our intention to notify national media interests and initiate legal proceedings should this matter not be handled in a timely manner and in total compliance with our request.

Likewise, steps would be taken if the church or its membership takes any efforts to embarrass, harass, harm or defame our family in any way because of this request.

Our goal as a family is to strengthen our relationship with God individually and collectively. We believe that the spiritual welfare of our family is at stake and is the primary concern and reason for this request.

We believe that God loves all of His people and cannot be lobbied by special interest groups for a better seat in His kingdom. We believe a church should not be a hotel for perfect saints, but a hospital for those in need of His healing. May God bless us all in our personal endeavors to follow Him.

Yours truly,

_____

Luke P. Kimball 03/09/1982

_____

Lucy R. Kimball 7/15/1983

_____

Stephen J. Kimball 09/10/2005

_____

Susan E. Kimball 06/24/2008

How Do We Know We Can Trust the Bible?

WHAT IS THE BIBLE?

The Bible is a compilation of 66 books that we call the "canon" (rule or standard) of Scripture. The Bible is divided into two sections: The **Old Testament** which covers the period of human history **from Creation to the Hebrew prophet Malachi in 400 B.C.**, and the **New Testament** which covers the period from the **Birth of Christ (4 A.D.) to the Revelation of John in 95 A.D**. The majority of the Old Testament was canonized long before Christ's birth with two marginal books being solidified into the final Jewish canon at the Council of Jamnia in 90 A.D. Most of the New Testament books were accepted by 100 A.D. with the exception of six debatable books that were officially recognized into the Christian canon at the Third Council of Carthage in 397 A.D.[1]

God is the supreme Author of biblical Scripture. 2 Timothy 3:16-17 states, **"All scripture is given by inspiration of God**, and *is* profitable for doctrine, for reproof, for correction, for instruction in righteousness: That the man of God may be perfect, throughly furnished unto all good works."**

When one considers the broad range of human contributors to the Bible from different time

---

[1] These six books are Hebrews, 2 Peter, James, 2 John, 3 John, and Revelation.

frames, various backgrounds, and completely different locations, writing on many controversial subjects, and yet all agreeing with one another, one can see the Divine origin of the Bible, for no book of human origin has ever accomplished this task. The following list of facts summarizes the uniqueness of this great book of Scripture:

WRITTEN OVER A PERIOD OF 1500 YEARS:

Old Testament = 39 Books in 3 Divisions (Written from Moses in 1400 B.C. to Malachi in 400 B.C.)
1. **Law (Torah):** Genesis, Exodus, Leviticus, Numbers, and Deuteronomy
2. **Prophets (Neviim):** Joshua, Judges, 1 & 2 Samuel, 1 & 2 Kings, Isaiah, Jeremiah, Ezekiel, and the 12 Minor Prophets (Hosea, Joel, Amos, Obadiah, Jonah, Micah, Nahum, Habakkuk, Zephaniah, Haggai, Zechariah, Malachi)
3. **Writings (Kethubim):** Psalms, Proverbs, Job, Ruth, Song of Solomon, Ecclesiastes, Lamentations, Esther, Daniel, Ezra, Nehemiah, 1 & 2 Chronicles

New Testament = 27 Books in 4 Divisions (Written from James in 45 A.D. to Revelation in 95 A.D.)
1. **Gospels:** Matthew, Mark, Luke, John
2. **History:** Acts
3. **Epistles:** Romans, 1 & 2 Corinthians, Galatians, Ephesians, Philippians, Colossians, 1 & 2 Thessalonians, 1 & 2

Timothy, Titus, Philemon, Hebrews, James, 1 & 2 Peter, 1, 2 & 3 John, Jude

4. **Prophecy**: Revelation

WRITTEN IN THREE LANGUAGES:

1. **Hebrew** = Most of the Old Testament Scriptures
2. **Aramaic** = Daniel 2-7:28; Jeremiah 10:11; Ezra 4-7; Matthew 27:46
3. **Koine Greek** = The New Testament (with the occasional exception of Aramaic phrases)

40 WRITERS FROM ALL WALKS OF LIFE - Living in many different places and encompassing three continents:

1. **Moses** = Genesis, Exodus, Leviticus, Numbers, Deuteronomy, Job
2. **Joshua** = Joshua
3. **Phinehas or Eleazar** = Portions of Joshua
4. **Samuel** = 1 & 2 Samuel, Judges, Ruth
5. **Nathan** = Portions of 1 & 2 Samuel
6. **Gad** = Portions of 1 & 2 Samuel
7. **Jeremiah** = 1 & 2 Kings, Jeremiah, Lamentations
8. **Ezra** = 1 Chronicles, 2 Chronicles, Ezra, Nehemiah
9. **Mordecai** = Esther
10. **David** = Most of Psalms
11. **Asaph** = Portions of Psalms
12. **Sons of Korah** = Portions of Psalms
13. **Heman the Ezrahite** = Portions of Psalms

14. **Ethan the Ezrahite** = Portions of Psalms
15. **Solomon** = Proverbs, Ecclesiastes, Song of Solomon, Portions of Psalms
16. **Agur son of Jakeh** = Portions of Proverbs
17. **Lemuel** = Portions of Proverbs
18. **Isaiah** = Isaiah
19. **Ezekiel** = Ezekiel
20. **Daniel** = Daniel
21. **Hosea** = Hosea
22. **Joel** = Joel
23. **Amos** = Amos
24. **Obadiah** = Obadiah
25. **Jonah** = Jonah
26. **Micah** = Micah
27. **Nahum** = Nahum
28. **Habakkuk** = Habakkuk
29. **Zephaniah** = Zephaniah
30. **Haggai** = Haggai
31. **Zechariah** = Zechariah
32. **Malachi** = Malachi
33. **Matthew** = Matthew
34. **Mark** = John Mark
35. **Luke** = Luke, Acts
36. **John** = John, 1 & 2 & 3 John, Revelation
37. **Paul** = Romans, 1 & 2 Corinthians, Galatians, Ephesians, Philippians, Colossians, 1 & 2 Thessalonians, 1 & 2 Timothy, Titus, Philemon, and possibly Hebrews (author unknown)
38. **James** = James
39. **Peter** = 1 & 2 Peter
40. **Jude** = Jude

HOW DO MORMONS VIEW THE BIBLE?

Mormons regard the King James Version of the Bible as Scripture but they add three books, that were "translated" and dictated by their founder, Joseph Smith, to complete their open canon of Scripture called "The Standard Works of the Church of Jesus Christ of Latter-day Saints." These additional Scripture books are the *Book of Mormon, Doctrine and Covenants,* and the *Pearl of Great Price.* Of these four books, the Bible is trusted the least. Although Mormons believe the Bible is an authoritative work of Scripture, they claim that many errors have crept into the text so that one cannot be sure that what is recorded in the Bible today is truly the Word of God as written by the Jewish prophets and apostles of biblical centuries. The eighth Article of Faith of the Church of Jesus Christ of Latter-day Saints states:

"We believe the **Bible to be the word of God as far as it is translated correctly**; we also believe the Book of Mormon to be the word of God."—*The Eighth Article of Faith, Pearl of Great Price*

Notice the qualification, "**as far as it is translated correctly,**" placed upon the Bible while no qualification is given to the text of the Book of Mormon. Joseph Smith declared that "ignorant translators, careless transcribers ...corrupt priests have committed many errors" in copying the text of the Bible.[2] Thus, Smith claimed that he restored and clarified the truths missing from the Bible through his publication of the Book of Mormon:

"I told the brethren that **the Book of Mormon was <u>the most correct of any book</u> on earth**, and the keystone of our religion, and a **man would get nearer to God by abiding by its precepts, than by any other book**."—*History of the Church, vol. 4, p. 461*

By claiming that the Book of Mormon stands apart from "any other book" as "the most correct of any book on earth," Joseph Smith placed the Book of Mormon above the Bible as the standard by which a "man would get nearer to God." If one is to believe Joseph's Smith's claim that the Book of Mormon is "the most correct" book on earth, one cannot help but question the integrity of the biblical text as one reads the wholesale attack upon the Bible's accuracy found in the pages of the Book of Mormon. **Seven times in the space of seven verses** quoted below from **First Nephi chapter thirteen,** the Book of Mormon dogmatically asserts, **"there are many plain and precious things taken away from the book, which is the book of the Lamb of God."**

"And the angel of the Lord said unto me: Thou hast beheld that **the book** proceeded

---

[2] *Teachings of the Prophet Joseph Smith*, 1976, by Joseph Fielding Smith, p. 327.

forth from the mouth of a Jew; and **when it proceeded forth from the mouth of a Jew it contained the fulness of the gospel of the Lord**, of whom the twelve apostles bear record; and they bear record according to the truth which is in the Lamb of God. **Wherefore, these things go forth from the Jews in purity unto the Gentiles**, according to the truth which is in God. **And after they go forth** by the hand of the twelve apostles of the Lamb, from the Jews unto the Gentiles, **thou seest the formation of that great and abominable church**, which is most abominable above all other churches; for behold, **they have <u>taken away from the gospel of the Lamb</u> <u>many parts which are plain and most precious</u>; and also many <u>covenants of the Lord have they taken away</u>**. ...Wherefore, thou seest that after the book hath gone forth through the hands of the great and abominable church, that **there are many plain and precious things <u>taken away from the book</u>, which is <u>the book of the Lamb of God</u>**. And after these **plain and precious things were <u>taken away</u>** it goeth forth unto all the nations of the Gentiles; and ...because of the **many plain and precious things which have been <u>taken out</u> of the book**...because of these things which are **<u>taken away</u> <u>out of the gospel of the Lamb</u>**, an exceedingly great many do stumble, yea, insomuch that Satan hath great power over them. ...Neither will the Lord God suffer that the Gentiles shall forever remain in that awful state of blindness, which thou beholdest they are in, because of the **plain and most precious parts of the gospel of the Lamb which have been kept back by that abominable church**, whose formation thou hast seen. ...the Gentiles do **stumble exceedingly, because of the most plain and precious parts of the gospel of the Lamb which have been kept back by that abominable church**, which is the mother of harlots, saith the Lamb.—I will be merciful unto the Gentiles in that day, insomuch that **I will bring forth unto them, in mine own power, much of my gospel, which shall be plain and precious, saith the Lamb**."—1 Nephi 13:24-26, 28-29, 32, 34

Although the Book of Mormon adamantly stresses that precious truths were "taken away" and "kept back" from the "gospel of the Lamb" by the "great and abominable church," it makes no attempt to "restore" these alleged lost truths. **There is not a single doctrine revealed in the Book of Mormon that is not already mentioned in the Bible.** Not only is there no sign of the so-called "plain and most precious parts of the gospel of the Lamb" that are allegedly missing from the Bible, but gone from the Book of Mormon are many of the unique doctrines of the Mormon gospel—such as baptism for the dead, the three degrees of glory, celestial marriage, God having a body of flesh and bones and the Word of Wisdom (food and drink law of Mormonism). These are all requirements that the LDS Church claims are necessary for a Mormon to be exaltated into the highest degree of Heaven, yet they are missing from the "precepts" of the book that Joseph Smith claimed would get a man "nearer to God...than...any other book." Furthermore, Jesus in the Book of Mormon warns against adding to His doctrines when He says:

> "Verily, verily, I say unto you, that **this is my doctrine**...and **whoso shall declare more or less than this, and establish it for my doctrine, the same cometh of evil**..."—3 Nephi 11:39-40[3]

Is the Mormon Church guilty of declaring "more...than" Jesus' doctrine by adding "precepts" not found in the Book of Mormon? You be the judge. In the meantime, we must ask why the Book of Mormon not only fails to "restore" these missing doctrines of Mormonism, but it contradicts the words of Jesus Christ, the true Lamb of God, who promised:

> "Heaven and earth shall pass away, but **my words shall not pass away**." —Matthew 24:35[4]

Who are we to believe? **Are we to believe Joseph Smith and the Book of Mormon that claim that "plain and precious parts" of**

---

[3] Compare this with Galatians 1:6-9 in the Bible.
[4] See also Mark 13:31 and Luke 21:33.

Jesus' words passed away? Or should we believe Jesus' promise to preserve His words? Jesus wasn't the only one in the Bible to promise that God's words would not be lost, the Prophet Isaiah made the following promise in the Old Testament and the Apostle Peter reiterated this promise in the New Testament:

> "The grass withereth, the flower fadeth: but the word of our God **shall stand for ever**."—Isaiah 40:8

> "But the **word of the Lord endureth for ever**. And this is the word which by the gospel is preached unto you."—1 Peter 1:25

JOSEPH SMITH'S INSPIRED VERSION OF THE BIBLE

In spite of God's promise that His Word would not be lost, Joseph Smith went so far as to produce his own version of the Bible in which he added hundreds of words to the text of Scripture without manuscript support whatsoever. His translation is called *The Inspired Version of the Bible* or *The Joseph Smith Translation (JST)*. The Mormon Church published some of Smith's revisions in the footnotes and appendix of its LDS version of the King James Bible and all of Smith's revisions are currently published in the book entitled, *Joseph Smith's "New Translation" of the Bible,* by Herald Publishing House owned by the Community of Christ (formerly the Reorganized Church of Jesus Christ of Latter Day Saints or RLDS).

Although Joseph Smith claimed that he finished his translation of the Scriptures in July of 1833,[5] most Mormons think that he did not finish it because the LDS Church has never published a full manuscript of it. Yet, not only did Joseph Smith testify to his completion of the Scriptures, he proclaimed that God commanded that his Bible translation should be printed.

".... the second lot on the south shall be dedicated unto me for the building of a house unto me, **for the work of the printing of the translation of my scriptures.**" —*Doctrine and Covenants,* 94:10

"And for this purpose I have commanded you to organize yourselves, even **to print my words, the fullness of my scriptures, the revelations which I have given unto you.**" —*Doctrine and Covenants,* 104:58

"...let him [William Law] from henceforth hearken to the counsel of my servant Joseph, ...and **publish the new translation of my holy word** unto the inhabitants of the earth." —*Doctrine and Covenants,* 124:89

If Joseph Smith never finished translating his Bible Scriptures as many Mormons today

---

[5] See *History of the Church,* vol.1, pp. 324, 368.

claim, what was Smith doing with so many revelations allegedly from God stating that he should print his Bible Scriptures? (See *Ensign,* January 1983). **Why would God command Joseph Smith to print an unfinished translation?** Despite revelations that claim that God commanded that Smith's Bible translation should be printed, the Mormon Church has never printed a full manuscript of it. Why? The LDS Church does not own the copyright to it. When Joseph Smith died and Brigham Young took over the leadership of the LDS Church, Joseph Smith's first wife Emma refused to give the manuscript to Young and instead gave it to a group called the Reorganized Church of Jesus Christ of Latter Day Saints led by her son who in turn published Smith's translation in 1867.

It is fascinating to study Joseph Smith's Translation of the Bible because **one will discover many changes and alterations that he made to the text of Scripture to validate his own unique views**. Some of the significant doctrinal changes Smith inserted into the text of his Bible are as follows:

- **KJV Romans 4:5:** "...believeth on him that **justifieth the ungodly**..."
- **JST Romans 4:5:** "...believeth on him who **justifieth _not_ the ungodly**..."[6]

---

[6] Smith's additions to the text of the Bible are noted in this and other quotations in italics. The insertion of the subtle word "not" into this text of Romans 4:5 completely changes the meaning of the passage and nullifies the Biblical doctrine of justification by faith alone that the Apostle Paul emphasized throughout Romans.

- **KJV Exodus 33:20:** "Thou canst not see my face: for **there shall no man see me, and live**."

- **JST Exodus 33:20:** "Thou canst not see my face *at this time*, *lest mine anger be kindled against thee also, and I destroy thee, and they people;* for there shall **no man among them see me** *at this time*, and live, *for they are exceeding sinful. And no sinful man hath at any time, neither shall there be any sinful man at any time, that shall see my face and live*."[7]

Joseph Smith even added an entire section to his Bible consisting of 15 verses and **over 800 words** between Genesis 50:24-26 to create a prophecy about himself. The following verse where he mentions himself by name is taken from this prophecy that Smith added to Genesis chapter fifty:

> "*And that seer will I bless, and they that seek to destroy him shall be confounded; for this promise I give unto you; for I will remember you from generation to generation; and* **his name shall be called Joseph, and it shall be after the name of his father**; *and he shall be like unto you; for the thing which the Lord shall bring forth by his hand shall bring my people*

---

[7] This qualification of disallowing a "sinful man" from seeing God's face, rather than ALL mankind, was changed to justify Smith's claim to see God the Father in his 1820 First Vision account.

unto salvation."—Genesis 50:33, Joseph Smith Translation

Joseph Smith's "Inspired Version" creates many difficulties for the LDS Church, not only because the Church violated the revelations of *Doctrine and Covenants* when it didn't print the full version of it, but also because **Smith's version does not correct the most problematic biblical Scriptures** that condemn the heretical beliefs of Mormonism. Verses such as Isaiah 44:6 and 8 that condemn Smith's "plurality of gods" concept[8] and Isaiah 43:10 that condemns the Mormon idea that men can become gods[9] are left intact in Joseph Smith's translation. Likewise, Joseph Smith's version makes no attempt to restore the alleged "missing books" that Mormons claim were removed from the Bible.

Finally, in the **thousands of manuscripts of the Bible that have been uncovered, some dating as far back as the 2nd Century B.C., not a single manuscript supports the changes that Joseph Smith made to the text of his Bible**. If the "plain and most precious parts of the gospel of the Lamb" were truly "taken away" and "kept back" **by the "abominable church"** of the middle ages, as the Book of Mormon claims,[10] why is such evidence completely missing from the manuscripts that we possess

---

[8] See *Teachings of the Prophet Joseph Smith,* 1976, by Joseph Fielding Smith, p. 370.
[9] See *Teachings of the Prophet Joseph Smith,* pp. 345-346.
[10] See 1 Nephi 13:24-26, 28-29, 32, 34.

today of the Holy Bible that date prior to the formation of the Catholic Church? Why is it that Smith's changes disagree with the manuscripts that the Book of Mormon says were pure at that time?[11] Such discrepancies between Smith's translation and the ancient manuscripts only suspect Joseph Smith of serious fraud and deception.

"Every word of God *is* pure: he *is* a shield unto them that put their trust in him. **Add thou not unto his words**, lest he reprove thee, and **thou be found a liar**." —Proverbs 30:5-6

HOW THE BIBLE WAS TRANSMITTED TO OUR DAY

Since the Bible was written over a period of fifteen hundred years, two to three thousand years before the invention of the printing press, **it was preserved through the process of handwriting and copying manuscripts** onto a variety of materials: **Papyrus** (most common ancient writing material made from papyrus reeds), **Parchment** (prepared skins of sheep, goats and other animals), **Vellum** (prepared from calf skins, often dyed purple and written upon with gold or silver), **Ostraca** (unglazed pottery), **Clay tablets** (engraved when wet and dried to make a permanent record), **Stones** (inscribed with an iron pen), and **Wax tablets** (flat wood

---

[11] See 1 Nephi 13:24-25.

covered with wax).[12] Due to the availability of papyrus, parchments, and vellum, most ancient manuscripts we possess of the Scriptures today consist of these materials and were prepared into either a scroll (a roll) or a codex (book form). Although we possess thousands of copies of the ancient manuscripts of the Bible, none of the original autographs have survived to our day.

Throughout the centuries, multiple translations of the manuscripts have been made into other languages. Thus, as noted earlier, the LDS Church's Eighth Article of Faith states that Mormons "believe the **Bible to be the word of God as far as it is translated correctly**." Upon hearing the phrase "translation," one might naïvely assume that a Mormon's concerns about the accuracy of the Bible could easily be satisfied by utilizing the many Greek and Hebrew resources available to compare the original Greek, Hebrew, and Aramaic text of the Bible against the modern language translations of the Bible that we posses today. While this would be a fairly easy task to undertake with the proper tools, it would not satisfy the Mormon's doubts about the Bible's accuracy because their concerns stem from a misunderstanding about the process by which the Bible was transmitted from one generation to another.

Many Mormons mistakenly assume that because scholars do not possess the original manuscripts of the Bible today, **they believe it is impossible**

---

[12] See *The New Evidence that Demands A Verdict*, 1999, by Josh McDowell, pp. 17-18.

to know what the original writers of the Bible wrote. They inaccurately attribute the phase "to translate the Bible" as a process by which they think the Bible was translated from one language to another language, to yet another language and so forth from one language to the next until we come to today's English version of the King James Bible. With this view of Bible transmission, one can easily understand how a Mormon can become convinced that **"many plain and precious"** doctrines of the Mormon gospel have been **"taken away from the book"**[13] of the Bible and apostate doctrines of Christianity substituted.

While this distorted view of Bible transmission may seem plausible, its erroneous conclusions become apparent when one considers the overwhelming manuscript evidence that proves the Bible has been preserved to **99.5% accuracy.** Although many "translations" of the biblical manuscripts have been made over the years, **the vast majority of these modern "translations" have relied upon copies made from the original language manuscripts.** Thus, "translations" made into other languages were only considered as a secondary source for understanding the meaning of difficult passages.

---

[13] 1 Nephi 13:28

THE PRESERVATION OF THE HEBREW OLD TESTAMENT MANUSCRIPTS

The Jews took the safeguarding of their Scriptures seriously. Thus, they trained special people called "scribes" to copy the Scriptures with great care and meticulously check and recheck for errors. Jewish scribes of the Masoretic era (500 A.D. to 950 A.D.) checked for errors in their copies by comparing the number of letters in the original manuscript with the number of letters in the copy and verifying whether the middle letter of the original document agreed with the middle letter of the copy. If the slightest discrepancy was found in the copy, it was rejected and the process of copying the original manuscript started over from scratch. It was through this process of scribal care that the accuracy of the Hebrew Old Testament manuscripts was preserved.

The earliest **complete manuscript copy of the Hebrew Old Testament that we possess today is the *Leningrad Codex (L)* dated at 1008 A.D.** Prior to the riots in Israel in 1947 when the *Aleppo Codex* **of 900 A.D.** was damaged, **it was the oldest complete Masoretic manuscript of the entire Old Testament**. These manuscripts along with partial manuscripts that we possess of the Hebrew Old Testament Scriptures dating from the 8th to the 10th Centuries form the basis of the **Hebrew Masoretic Text from which all**

Bible versions today are translated.[14]   In 1947, when the dead Sea Scrolls were discovered in the Qumran caves, about 25 kilometers east of Jerusalem, fragments of all of the Old Testaments books (except for Esther) were found in these scrolls **dating back to the 2nd Century B.C.** The most significant find was a complete Hebrew copy of the book of Isaiah. When this scroll from the 2nd Century B.C. was compared with the oldest known text of Isaiah from approximately 900 A.D., scholars were amazed to find the text of Isaiah virtually unchanged with 95% accuracy in over 1,000 years of copying! The majority of the 5% variations between the manuscripts consisted chiefly of slips of the pen and obvious spelling errors that did not affect the message of the text.[15]   Thus, one can have confidence in the accuracy of the Hebrew manuscripts that scholars use today to translate the Old Testament portion of our Bible into the modern languages of today.

THE PRESERVATION OF THE GREEK NEW TESTAMENT MANUSCRIPTS

While the Jews assigned the task of copying the manuscripts of the Old Testament to trained scribes, the New Testament Christian Church did not have this process for their Scriptures. Rather, as the New Testament Scriptures

---

[14] See *Old Testament Textual Criticism—A Practical Introduction,* 1994, by Ellis R. Brotzman, pp. 56-57 and *The New Evidence That Demands A Verdict,* p. 73.
[15] See *The New Evidence That Demands A Verdict,* pp. 70, 90.

circulated among the churches of the first century, individuals indiscriminately made copies for personal and congregational use. Thus, minor discrepancies proliferated between the copies just as one would expect when precision in copying is not emphasized to the extent that it was by the Hebrew scribes.

Most of these discrepancies (textual variants) consist of minor spelling errors that are easily recognized by the scholar and the incidental addition or deletion of a marginal note that often has no bearing upon the overall message of the script. In most cases, a comparison of multiple manuscript copies can easily determine the original author's intent.

Scholars today have over 24,000 partial and complete manuscripts of the New Testament from which to compare texts. **5,686 of these manuscripts are in Greek** and **19,284 are ancient language translations**. Most of the Greek manuscripts were copied between the 9th to the 16th Century, several hundred copied between the 4th to the 8th Centuries, and a few ancient papyrus manuscripts date back to the 2nd and 3rd Century. The oldest manuscript is Papyrus 52 (P52) of the gospel of John, copied at 125 A.D.

The oldest manuscript of the complete New Testament is the Greek Codex Sinaiticus from 325 A.D. It along with the Codex Vaticanus, also from the 4th Century, form the basis of **Brook Foss Westcott** and **Fenton**

John Anthony Hort's *The New Testament in the Original Greek* of 1881. These manuscripts contain not only the entire Greek New Testament but a large portion of the Greek Septuagint Translation of the Hebrew Old Testament which was preserved in them as well. Thus, together these manuscripts are considered **the oldest manuscripts that we possess today of the entire Bible in Greek**. The following charts, adapted from Josh McDowell's *New Evidence That Demands a Verdict,*[16] provides a breakdown of the total number of surviving New Testament manuscripts available today:

Extant Greek Manuscripts	No. of Copies
Uncials (All Capital Letters)	307
Minuscules (Upper and Lower Case)	2,860
Lectionaries	2,410
Papyri	109
SUBTOTAL	**5,686**

Manuscripts in Other Languages	No. of Copies
Latin Vulgate	10,000
Ethiopic	2,000
Slavic	4,107
Armenian	2,587
Syriac Pashetta	350
Bohairic	100
Arabic	75
Old Latin	50
Anglo Saxon	7
Gothic	6
Sogdian	3
Old Syriac	2

---

[16] *The New Evidence That Demands A Verdict,* p. 34.

Persian	2
Frankish	1
SUBTOTAL	**19,284**
GRAND TOTAL (with NT Greek)	**24,970**

Compare these manuscript totals with that of any other book of antiquity and you will discover that there are no ancient manuscripts that compare to the manuscript support we have for our New Testament text. This is demonstrated by the following chart from Josh McDowell's New Evidence That Demands a Verdict:[17]

AUTHOR	BOOK	DATE WRITTEN	EARLIEST COPY	TIME GAP	NO. OF COPIES
Homer	*Iliad*	800 B.C.	400 B.C.	400 Years	643
Herodotus	*History*	480-425 B.C.	900 A.D.	1,350 Years	8
Plato	*The Republic*	400 B.C.	900 A.D.	1,300 years	7
Caesar	*Gallic Wars*	100-44 B.C.	900 A.D.	1,000 years	10
Livy	*History of Rome*	59 B.C. – 17 A.D.	4th Century (Partial) 10th Century	400 years 1,000 years	1 partial 19 copies
Tacitus	*Annals*	100 A.D.	1,100 A.D.	1,000 years	20
Pliny Secundus	*Natural History*	61-113 A.D.	850 A.D.	750 years	7
New Testament		50-100 A.D.	114 A.D. (fragments) 200 A.D. (full books) 325 A.D. (Complete)	+ 50 years 100 years 225 years	**5,686 partial and complete**

---

[17] *The New Evidence That Demands A Verdict,* p. 38.

THE NEW TESTAMENT PRESERVED IN QUOTATIONS FROM THE CHURCH FATHERS

Quotations of the New Testament Scriptures from **seven early church fathers**[18] starting with **Justin Martyr** (100 A.D.) to **Eusebius of Caesarea** (339 A.D.) number **36,289 by the time period of the Council of Nicea.** As if this number of early church father quotations of the New Testament were not impressive enough, one could add the quotations of church fathers contemporary with **Augustine of Hippo** (354 A.D) and many subsequent fathers to **come up with a total of 86,489 quotations.**[19]   Josh McDowell notes:

> "...the quotations are so numerous and widespread that **if no manuscripts of the New Testament were extant, the New Testament could be reproduced from the writings of the early Fathers alone.** (Geisler, GIB, 430)   In brief, J. Harold Greenlee was right when he wrote, 'These quotations are so extensive that the **New Testament could virtually be reconstructed** from them **without the use of New Testament Manuscripts.'** (Greenlee, INTTC, 54)" —*The New Evidence That Demands a Verdict,* p. 43

---

[18] The seven church fathers counted in this total are: Justin Martyr, Irenaeus, Clement of Alexandria, Origen, Tertullian, Hippolytus, Eusebius of Caesarea referenced in *The New Evidence That Demands A Verdict,* p. 43.

[19] *The New Evidence That Demands A Verdict,* p. 45.

Indeed, manuscript support for the New Testament Scriptures leaves no doubt of the fact that we posses today **all of the content** in the original Scriptures dictated by the Prophets and Apostles of our first century faith.

HOW SCHOLARS OF THE GREEK NEW TESTAMENT RESOLVE TEXTUAL DISCREPANCIES

Mormons often contend that textual variants (discrepancies) between the manuscripts of the Scriptures prove that the Bible is inaccurate. This accusation is simply not correct, as we will demonstrate by our examination of the process by which textual scholars scrutinize multiple copies of the Scriptural manuscripts to determine the essential meaning behind the variants.

Our first example is **Desiderius Erasmus** (1466-1536) who studied six partial Greek manuscripts of the New Testament to create a single manuscript called the ***Textus Receptus*** (Received Text) that formed the basis of the New Testament portion of the 1611 King James Version of the Bible. He evaluated the variants in these manuscripts to determine which renderings were most correct. One of the passages to which he gave considerable attention was **1 John 5:7-8.** The Latin Vulgate of the Middle Ages added many words to the text that is unsupported by the Greek manuscripts.

This textual variant is now called the **Comma Johanneum** and in the Old Latin Vulgate it read:

LATIN: *"testimonium dicunt* [or *dant*] *in terra, spiritus* [or: *spiritus et*] *aqua et sanguis, et hi tres unum sunt in Christo Iesu. et tres sunt, qui testimonium dicunt in caelo, pater verbum et spiritus."*

1 JOHN 5:7-8:

LATIN VULGATE OF THE MIDDLE AGES	MODERN TRANSLATION (NASB)
"For there are three giving evidence on earth, spirit, water and blood, and these three are one **in Christ Jesus. And the three, which give evidence in heaven, are father word and spirit**."[20]	"For there are three that testify: the Spirit and the water and the blood; and the three are in agreement."

Because the Latin Vulgate was the common Bible of his day, Desiderius Erasmus received much criticism when his first and second editions of his Greek **manuscript did not contain the extra words of the Comma Johanneum.** His critics accused Erasmus of

---

[20] The Latin and English translation of the Middle Ages' version of the Latin Vulgate at 1 John 5:7-8 is taken from the Wikipedia website at http://en.wikipedia.org/wiki/Comma_Johanneum as the Latin Vulgate of today has been changed to agree with the modern translations in excluding the additional words of the *Comma Johanneum.*

supporting the heretical belief of "Arianism" that denied the Trinity and taught that Jesus was not God. Since Erasmus was unable to find a single Greek manuscript that supported these additional words, his note in the *Annotations* of his first two Greek text editions read:

> "In the Greek codex I find only this about the threefold testimony: 'because there are three witnesses, spirit, water, and blood.'"[21]

When Erasmus challenged his critics to present him with a Greek manuscript that supported the rendering of the *Comma Johanneum* at 1 John 5:7-8, they presented Erasmus with an Irish manuscript (Codex Montfortianus) that many believe was fabricated and translated into Greek at this passage from the Latin Vulgate itself. Remaining true to his word, Erasmus reluctantly inserted the *Comma Johanneum* into his third edition of the *Textus Receptus* with the following note:

> "I have restored the text... so as not to give anyone an occasion for slander."[22]

To this day, the *Textus Receptus* and all Bible translations based upon this manuscript (i.e., the *King James Version* and the *New King James Version*), contain the additional words of the *Comma Johanneum*, while all other translations

---

[21] Quoted from *The King James Only Controversy*, 1995, James R. White, p. 60.

[22] Quoted from *The King James Only Controversy* p. 61.

exclude it based upon the evidence of thousands of manuscripts (including the Codex Sinaiticus and Codex Vaticanus) that all exclude the *Comma Johanneum* from their texts.

Times have changed from the days of Erasmus's half dozen Greek manuscripts. Scholars now have over 24,000 partial and complete manuscripts of the New Testament from which to compare texts. Given the availability of thousands of manuscripts, it is easy for modern scholars to determine what the original authors of the New Testament manuscripts wrote in their texts. While we have discussed the *Comma Johanneum* which is one of the more critical textual variants of the New Testament, most variants are incidental and have no bearing upon the general meanings of the text. Some of these variants are as follows:

KING JAMES VERSION	NEW AMERICAN STANDARD BIBLE
ACTS 16:7: "...the **Spirit** suffered them not."	**ACTS 16:7:** "...the Spirit of Jesus **did not permit them.**"
ACTS 22:16: "...wash away thy sins, calling on the **name of the Lord**."	**ACTS 22:16: "...wash away your sins, calling on** His name."
PHILIPPIANS 4:13: "I can do all things through **Christ** which strengtheneth me."	**PHILIPPIANS** 4:13: **"I can do all things through** Him **who strengthens me."**
1 PETER 3:15: "But sanctify the **Lord God** in your hearts..."	**1 PETER 3:15:** "But sanctify **Christ as Lord** in your hearts..."

As noted in the examples given in the above chart, most of the textual variants have to do with the addition or exclusion of the words "God," "Jesus", or "Christ" to the word "Lord" or "Spirit" or the substitute personal pronoun of "Him" for "Christ" in the manuscripts. Although the majority of the oldest Greek manuscripts favor the rendering of modern translations, such as the *New American Standard Bible* illustrated above, none of the variant renderings change the inherent meanings of the text. Through comparison, such as these illustrated above, one can easily determine the essential message of the original authors of the New Testament. Thus, as Norman L. Geisler and Frank Turek note:

> "Textual scholars **Westcott and Hort estimated** that only *one in sixty* of these variants has significance. **This would leave a text 98.33 percent pure**... **No ancient book is so well authenticated**. The great New Testament scholar and Princeton professor **Bruce Metzger** estimated that the *Mahabharata* of Hinduism is copied with only about 90 percent accuracy and Homer's *Illiad* with about 95 percent. **By comparison, he estimated the New Testament is about 99.5 percent accurate**. Again, the 0.5 percent in question does not affect a single doctrine of the Christian faith."—*I Don't Have Enough Faith to Be an Atheist*, 2004, p. 229

IS THE BIBLE MISSING BOOKS?

Mormons often point to the names of books cited in the Bible, not found in the text of Scripture, as evidence that the Bible's Scripture is incomplete. Some of the common books mentioned in the Bible that Mormons consider "lost" or "missing" are as follows:

- The book of the wars of the Lord (Numbers 21:14).
- The book of Jasher (Joshua 10:13; 2 Samuel 1:18).
- The book of the manner of the kingdom (1 Samuel 10:25).
- The acts or annals of Solomon (1 Kings 11:41).
- The book of Gad the Seer (1 Chronicles 29:29).
- The book of Nathan the prophet (1 Chronicles 29:29; 2 Chronicles 9:29).
- The book of Jehu (2 Chronicles 20:34).
- The book of Enoch (Jude 14)
- An earlier epistle of Paul to the Ephesians (Ephesians 3:3)
- An earlier epistle of Paul to the Corinthians (1 Corinthians 5:9);
- An epistle to the Colossians written from Laodicea (Colossians 4:16).

It is important to note first of all that these books were not "lost" from the Bible. These books were common knowledge to the people of their day and some have even survived down to our day, like the book of Enoch listed above.

227

The reason they are not found in our Bible is because they were never considered Scripture in the first place! Mormons incorrectly assume that if a book is mentioned in the text of Scripture, that book itself must also be considered Scripture as well. This is a false assumption because most of the unscriptural books mentioned in the Bible were merely journals of the prophets and the seers or historical books, like the "book of the wars of the LORD" mentioned at Numbers 21:14. **There is nothing in the text of Scripture that indicates that God intended these unscriptural books to be preserved in His Holy Word, the Bible.** Furthermore, when one examines these books that have been preserved to our day (like the book of Enoch), one finds that these books lack divine authority and/or contain inaccuracies in the text that prevent them from being canonized into the Scriptures. This is why none of the unscriptural books mentioned in the Bible were considered Scripture by the people of their day. However, it is worth discussing the alleged missing epistles of Paul as most of his epistles (unlike the other books in the list above) are considered Scripture.

Was Paul's letter of mystery lost (Ephesians 3:3-4)?

At Ephesians 3:3-4, Paul makes mention of an earlier writing in which **he discussed the mystery that God made known to him by a revelation.** It is important to realize that Paul's letters did not always stay with the particular church addressed, but were often copied and circulated among other churches. This was certainly true of the book of Ephesians as Paul wrote this letter with the specific intention of circulating it to all of the churches of Asia Minor. Thus, it is quite possible that the "revelation" of the "mystery" that Paul wrote about earlier is a reference to an earlier letter, possibly 1 Corinthians where Paul wrote about the "mystery" of God (1 Corinthians 2:7-10) "in few words" (Ephesians 3:3). Since Paul wrote 1 Corinthians from the city of Ephesus (1 Corinthians 16:8), it is quite reasonable to conclude that the Ephesians still had access to a copy of this Corinthian letter that Paul wrote during his stay there.

Was Paul's first letter to the Corinthians lost (1 Corinthians 5:9)?

At 1 Corinthians 5:9, Paul stated, "I wrote unto you in an epistle not to company with fornicators." Regarding this passage, Norman Geisler and Thomas Howe comment:

> "There are three possibilities here. **First, it may be that not all apostolic letters were intended to be in the canon of Scripture**. Luke refers to "many" other gospels (1:1). John implies that there was much more Jesus did that was not recorded (20:30; 21:25). Perhaps this so called 'lost' letter to the Corinthians was not intended by God to be collected in the canon and preserved...

"**Second, others believe that the letter referred to (in 1 Cor. 5:9) may not be lost at all, but is part of an existing book in the Bible**. For example, it could be part of what we know as 2 Corinthians (chaps. 10-13), which some believe was later put together with chapters 1-9. In support of this is offered the fact that chapters 1-9 have a decidedly different tone from the rest of the Book of 2 Corinthians (chapters 10-13). This may indicate that it was written on a different occasion... They also note that Paul refers to 'letters' (plural) he had written in 2 Corinthians 10:10.

"Third, others believe that Paul is referring to the present Book of 1 Corinthians in 1 Corinthians 5:9, that is, to the very book which he was writing at the time. In support of this they note ...Even though the Greek aorist tense used here ('I wrote') may refer to a past letter, it could also refer to the book at hand. This is called an 'epistolary aorist,' because it refers to the very book in which it is being used."
—*When Critics Ask - Popular Handbook on Bible Difficulties,* 1992, pp. 152-153

Was Paul's epistle from Laodicea lost (Colossians 4:16)?

At Colossians 4:16, Paul commands the church at Colossae, "When this epistle is read among you, cause that it be read also in the church of the Laodiceans; and that **ye likewise read the epistle <u>from Laodicea</u>**." Some argue that the "epistle from Laodicea" is a lost letter of Paul because none of Paul's letters in our New Testament bear this title. However, the text says this letter was "from Laodicea" — not that the letter was called by that name. There is good evidence that the letter "from Laodicea" is a reference to the book of Ephesians. There are several reasons for this. First, Paul wrote Ephesians at the same time that he wrote the book of Colossians. Second, Ephesians was a kind of cyclical letter that Paul sent throughout the churches of Asia Minor, and three early Greek manuscripts do not contain the words "at Ephesus" in Ephesians 1:1 in the phrase, "to the saints which are at Ephesus." Thus, many believe that the letter coming "from Laodicea" mentioned in Colossians 4:16 was in fact a reference to Paul's Ephesian letter.[23]

IS THE BOOK OF MORMON MISSING BOOKS?

While Mormons are quick to assert that cited books not included in the text of Scripture are proof that the Bible is incomplete, they fail to apply this same standard to their Book of Mormon which has no less than 10 books cited that are not included in its text. Are we to argue that the Book of Mormon is incomplete because these books are not included? No Mormon would agree to this.

---

[23] See *When Critics Ask - Popular Handbook on Bible Difficulties,* 1992, by Norman Geisler and Thomas Howe, p. 489.

- Book of Remembrance (3 Nephi 24:16)
- Prophecies of Zenos (1 Nephi 19:10; Jacob 5:1)
- Prophecies of Zenock (1 Nephi 19:10)
- Prophecies of Neum (1 Nephi 19:10)
- Missing Plates from Laban (1 Nephi 3:3-4)
- Lost Teachings of Benjamin (Mosiah 1:8)
- Lost Word of Amulek (Alma 9:34)
- Lost Words of Alma (Alma 13:31)
- Lost Teachings of Alma (Alma 8:1)
- Lost Teachings of Helaman (Helaman 5:13)

We must remember that God the Father and Jesus Christ Himself promised that the Word of God would endure forever.[24] Thus, if one book of Scripture were lost, we would have to question the strength of God to keep His promises. Indeed, such is not the case for Scripture declares that **God cannot lie** (Titus 1:2)!

IS THE BIBLE COMPLETE OR SHOULD WE LOOK FOR NEW REVELATION?

Mormons boast in the ability of their LDS prophets to reveal new Scripture to the church today. Thus, their canon of four Scripture books is never considered closed, but the "inspired words" of living LDS prophets become "scripture" to them as well.[25] Just as a child boasts of his "new" toys to his playmates, so Mormons boast of their "new" revelation from

---

[24] See Isaiah 40:8; Matthew 24:35; 1 Peter 1:25.
[25] See Gospel Principles, 1995 p. 55.

the Book of Mormon that taunts Christians who cling to the "old" revelations of the Bible:

"And because my words shall hiss forth—**many of the Gentiles shall say: A Bible! A Bible! We have got a Bible, and there cannot be any more Bible.** ...**Thou fool, that shall say: A Bible, we have got a Bible, and we need no more Bible.** Have ye obtained a Bible save it were by the Jews? Know ye not that there are more nations than one?"—2 Nephi 29:3, 6-7

To respond to these accusations, Christians often look for a verse from the Bible that teaches that the canon of Scripture was closed at Revelation—the final book of the New Testament. Unfortunately, this Scripture does not exist, although **many often incorrectly appeal to Revelation 22:18-19**:

"For I testify unto every man that heareth the words of the prophecy of this book, **If any man shall add unto these things**, God shall add unto him the plagues that are written in this book: And **if any man shall take away from the words of the book of this prophecy, God shall take away his part out of the book of life**, and out of the holy city, and *from* the things which are written in this book."

In context, Revelation 22:18-19 refers to the book of Revelation, not to the Bible as a whole. Although no Scripture speaks of the fact that the canon of Scripture was closed with writing of the last book of the Bible, Scripture does claim that "all the counsel of God" has been declared and that God has already given us "all things" that pertain to life and godliness:

"For I have not shunned to declare unto you **all the counsel of God**."—Acts 20:27

"According as his divine power **hath given unto us all things that *pertain* unto life and godliness**, through the knowledge of him that hath called us to glory and virtue."—2 Peter 1:3

If "all things that pertain unto life and godliness" and "all the counsel of God" have already been declared to us through the Bible, what need do we have of new "counsel" from God in the form of additional Scripture? As we have already proven, none of God's words have been lost, so there is no need for a "restoration" of "plain and precious" gospel truths through the Book of Mormon that LDS call "Scripture." Furthermore, in regard to the concept of receiving latter-day revelation, Biblical Scripture **gives the following strong warnings:**

1. Do not to "go beyond" what is written (1 Corinthians 4:6; 2 John 1:9).
2. Do not "add" or "take away" from the words God has spoken (Deuteronomy 4:2; Proverbs 30:6).

3. Do not contradict what God has recorded in Scripture (Isaiah 8:20; Deuteronomy 13:1-5).
4. Do not proclaim messages in God's name that He did not give (Deuteronomy 18:20-22).
5. Do not twist Scripture to fit your own distorted doctrines (2 Peter 3:16).

When one measures Latter-day (Mormon) "Scripture" against these guidelines, one finds that it fails on all five accounts. Fundamentally, it is an issue of whom you trust. Do you trust Joseph Smith and the Book of Mormon that claim that Jesus failed to keep His promise to preserve His Word (1 Nephi 13)? Or do you trust Jesus Christ and His promises (Matthew 24:35; Mark 13:31; Luke 21:33)? He warned:

> **"Beware of false prophets**, which come to you in sheep's clothing, but inwardly they are ravening wolves. **Ye shall know them by their fruits**."— Matthew 7:15-16

The "fruits" of this Mormon "false prophet" are evident. One cannot have it both ways, for to believe the Book of Mormon is to call Jesus a liar. MAY IT NEVER BE!

> "For what if some did not believe? Shall their unbelief make the faith of God without effect? God forbid: **yea, let God be true, but every man a liar**."—Romans 3:3-4

Leaving Mormonism
~ A New Life Awaits You!

Coming out of Mormonism was the single most significant, emotional and spiritual event that we had *ever gone through.* **We felt ALONE!** We knew of **NO ONE** who had left the Church! We had absolutely **no one** to talk to. We did not realize that there were thousands of Mormons who had left Mormonism after they had discovered that the Mormon Church was **not** what we had been taught it was.

Many deceitful things had transpired within Mormon history that **shocked** us! We had learned about blood atonement, Lying for the Lord, polygamy and polyandry. We learned how the Book of Mormon was translated using a rock in a hat and **not** by use of the gold plates as Mormonism had portrayed.

We were surprised to discover that there are nine different versions of the First Vision and that Joseph Smith did not even tell anyone about his vision of seeing God until 12 years after the fact. Then, reading the Book of Mormon and seeing with our own eyes how it disagreed with Mormon Scripture within the Doctrine and Covenants was disturbing to us. But we were most disgusted when we learned that what we were told about the Bible being corrupt and that it could not be trusted, was totally and completely false!

We fasted, we prayed, and we went to the temple only to find no comfort or support from our leaders. After years of trying to make sense of all that was going on within the Church of Jesus Christ of Latter-day Saints, we realized that we had been told Lies ... **TOTAL** Lies by our Church leaders as they tried to cover up the facts of Mormon history!

Then one day, it was as if we heard God yelling out:

> *"Can you hear Me? I've been trying to tell you to* **'LEAVE the MORMON Church.'** *This Church who call themselves, The Church of Jesus Christ of Latter-day Saints, is 'Another' gospel, other than what I taught! Even on the front of their Book of Mormon they proudly display the words,* **'Another** *Testament of Christ'."*

In **Galatians 1:6-10**, it reads:

> *" 6 I am astonished that you are so quickly deserting the one who called you to live in the grace of Christ and are turning to a* **different gospel** *(another gospel) — 7 which is really no gospel at all. Evidently some people are throwing you into confusion and are trying to pervert the gospel of Christ. 8 But even if we or an* **angel from heaven** *should preach a gospel other than the one we preached to you,* **let them be under God's curse!** *9 As we have already said, so now I say again: If anybody is preaching to*

you a gospel other than what you accepted, let them be under God's curse! 10 Am I now trying to win the approval of human beings, or of God? Or am I trying to please people? If I were still trying to please people, I would not be a servant of Christ."

We hope that you **know that you are NOT ALONE**! We are here to help you cross over into true Biblical Christianity!

Come to know the gospel of **Jesus Christ**, not the gospel of Joseph Smith. Come to know who Jesus Christ REALLY is! Who God REALLY is! Come to have a personal relationship with Jesus Christ! Know that we are here to help you as you come out of Mormonism into Christianity.

You can contact us directly through our website at LeeBaker.4Mormon.org. We would love to hear from you.

God Bless,
Kathy & Lee Baker

ABOUT THE AUTHOR

Christina Darlington is the founder of Witnesses for Jesus, a ministry to Jehovah's Witnesses and Latter-day Saints (Mormons). As a devoted Christian, her passion is to alert the Christian community to the un-Christian doctrines of these groups and to train and equip Christians to be effective witnesses to those ensnared by these counterfeit religions.

God is the God of truth, and truth does not fear examination. If a religious church cannot stand up under examination, it is not "the True Church," but is rather a counterfeit, and LOYALTY to a counterfeit is DISLOYALTY to God Himself. The ministry of Witnesses for Jesus was born out of a deep love and concern for Mormons who have committed their lives to a counterfeit faith.

> "But I am afraid, lest as the serpent deceived Eve by his craftiness, your minds should be led astray from the **simplicity** and **purity of devotion to Christ**. For if one comes and preaches **another Jesus** whom we have not preached ...you bear this beautifully."
> —2 Corinthians 11:3-4 (NASB)

> "**Test yourselves** to see if you are in the faith; examine yourselves! Or do you not recognize this about yourselves, that Jesus Christ is in you-unless indeed you fail the test?"
> —2 Corinthians 13:5 (NASB)

Exclusive religions like the Church of Jesus Christ of Latter-day Saints often refer to their religious faith as being the ultimate "truth" or the "only true Church." Because the members of these groups are taught that the only way to the highest level of heaven is through their particular faith, each person's identity and security is wrapped up in his or her religious affiliation with that faith.

Real truth, however, is not found in identifying with a particular religious faith or denomination, but in a personal relationship with Jesus, for He proclaims that He is THE TRUTH, and promises: *"you shall know the truth, and the truth shall make you free ... If therefore* **the Son shall make you free**, *you shall be free indeed ...* **I am the way, and the truth, and the life**; *no one comes to the Father, but through Me."* —*John 8:32, 36; 14:6 (NASB)*

"And the witness is this, that God has given us eternal life, and this life is in His Son. He who has the Son has the life; he who does not have the Son of God does not have the life. These things I have written to you who believe in the name of the Son of God, in order that you may know that you have eternal life."—*1 John 5:11-13 (NASB)*

WITNESSES FOR JESUS INC
PO BOX 50911
COLORADO SPRINGS, CO 80949 USA

4Witness.org * 4Mormon.org
LeeBaker.4Mormon.org

76779193R00140

Made in the USA
San Bernardino, CA
15 May 2018